# THE CARE AND FEEDING
# OF WHITE LIBERALS

# The
# Care and Feeding
# of
# White Liberals

*The American Tragedy*
*and the*
*Liberal Dilemma*

*by*

Hubert G. Locke

NEWMAN PRESS

New York, N.Y.  Paramus, N.J.
London  Toronto

# Contents

FOREWORD by Senator Edmund Muskie ............................... vii

INTRODUCTION ............................................................... 1

   I White Racism—Or What To Do Until We Find
     a Cure for This Madness ............................... 5

  II To Be Or Not To Be . . . A White Liberal ................. 15

 III Diagnosing the Disease ................................. 25

 IV Integration . . . Or the Death of an Idea ................ 35

  V Why Integration Failed . . . Or What We
    Discovered about Mediocrity ........................... 43

 VI So What Do We Do Next? (Guidelines for
    Black Radicals) ....................................... 53

VII Sex and the White Racist . . . Single, Married
    or Otherwise .......................................... 61

VIII The White Liberal as Conservative ...................... 71

EPILOGUE ................................................... 79

*This little book*
*is gratefully dedicated*
*to my parents*
*and my wife*
*who have saved me*
*from anger over the past*
*and despair in the present*
*and to my daughter*
*for whom I work*
*and pray*
*for a more decent future*

# Foreword

America is passing through a crisis in confidence. We are not certain that the ideals of our Declaration of Independence and the promises of our Constitution are close to reality. We are not at all certain that our democratic institutions can withstand the onslaught of the left and the right.

Part of that loss of confidence has been the product of the bitter division on the war in Vietnam. Part of it stems from the realization that our crowded, complex, and technologically dominated society doesn't work as well as it is supposed to. But one of the deepest causes of our concern has been the growing division between black and white Americans.

In the 1950's and the 1960's, black and white Americans joined in the assault on segregation and discrimination. Their number was small but their spirit was great. Together they staged sit-ins at segregated restaurants and movie theaters; together they crossed segregated school barriers; together they marched through Selma, Birmingham and Washington to gain attention and action.

There have been changes as a result of those efforts. But the changes have not been large enough or come fast enough to satisfy those who were oppressed and isolated from the benefits of our society.

More and more black Americans chafed at the assumption that their gains could come only at the hands of whites, just as their losses had been imposed by whites.

The result, amplified by continued resistance to the end of discrimination in many areas, has been a growing tension between former allies, and deepening suspicion on both sides of the color line. I suspect this development was inevitable, and not entirely unhealthy.

If we mean what we say about equality, then black Americans should not have to depend on white Americans to give them their rights. If we really believe in individual rights, then black Americans should not be criticized for asserting their individuality. But that is not the end of the story.

A democratic society may be a pluralistic society, but it cannot be a fragmented society. If it is to survive as a community in which each citizen has an opportunity to achieve his or her potential, it must have joint action toward common goals without regard to differences in color or ethnic origin. If the traditions of freedom are to be maintained, those traditions must be supported by trust and confidence between the members of society.

This is Hubert Locke's message, backed by a knowledge of the history of the civil rights movement, motivated by religious conviction and humane compassion, and given force by his commitment to a whole society. His is a thoughtful and moving book which should contribute to an end to the crisis in confidence in our society.

SENATOR EDMUND MUSKIE

# Introduction

This little book grew out of frequent forays into white suburbia, prolonged parlays with white liberal friends, and some rather agonizing and amusing appraisals of what is taking place in regard to the racial question in American society. It reflects a growing personal conviction that the plight of that much-maligned, ofttimes misunderstood and almost pathetic creature—the white liberal—is perhaps one of the great tragedies of our times. Like all tragedy, the white liberal dilemma is reflected in the apparent hopelessness of his situation; whichever way he moves, whatever choices he makes in trying to rectify America's racial wrongs, he seems to be doomed to failure.

But the liberal's plight also partakes of the pathetic; there is a sad touch of humor in his dismay and confusion, his thrashing about for new rhetoric and more effective programs. There is humor also, if not irony, in the fact that the white liberal is not listening to or learning from what is going on in contemporary America any more than the white racist whom he so righteously denounces. The liberal's faith in his liberal pronouncements have been damaged rather dramatically, but his confidence in his liberal pretensions remains unshaken; he clings as unswervingly as ever to pet theories of educating away bigotry and to projects like open housing.

Yet, America's white liberal cannot be written off as a relic of the past. Indeed his role may well prove to be pivotal for the America of the future. For unless we are prepared to settle for this country not simply becoming two nations, as the Kerner Report predicted, but two warring racial camps, which is infinitely and imminently more realistic, then we have to count on the basic good sense of decent-thinking white

1

Americans—the liberals, if you will—to pull the rest of their clan kicking and screaming into the 20th century, while we blacks try to sort out the pieces of the enormous social and cultural mess white America has bequeathed to us and attempt to lift our masses out of its debilitating and dehumanizing effects.

To do so calls for the mutual recognition that America is a sick nation, Eric Hoffer notwithstanding. (As any first-year medical student knows, a patient need not be violent in order to be seriously ill. If the patient is violent, it simply compounds the sickness.) Black folk have known this for generations; we've been quietly muttering to one another that something was "ailing white folk," but we didn't know exactly what (although we had strong suspicions) until the perceptive diagnosis of the Kerner Commission was made public two years ago. Black people thought that once the disease was identified, its victims would literally leap to find a cure. How wrong a guess that was! Most of the white populace has refused even to read the medical report, let alone ask the doctors for some curative relief. As a result, the faithful band of white liberals in the nation are left in an extraordinary state of frustration; like a small band of researchers who have discovered the virus that causes cancer, they find themselves unable to convince anyone that he has the disease.

Meanwhile the disease goes unchecked, and white liberals, finding that black Americans seem no longer interested in their reports of its devastating progress or their attempts—well meaning though they might be—to drag us into sick bay to see for ourselves how bad the illness is, and discovering simultaneously that their white constituencies are not the least bit anxious about their sickness but instead appear to be a bit defiant about it, are in a high state of confusion and despair. As unpopular (and perhaps unrealistic) as it may be, however, I am not prepared to give up on this valiant cadre of visionaries. To the contrary, I am convinced that liberals might make a stellar comeback if they ceased to treat racism as a social problem (and accordingly gave up on T-groups, role-playing, human relations councils, sensitivity training and the like) and tackled the matter with the insights and methods of modern medicine, a field in which we've had infinitely more success in finding answers to vexing situations.

Hence, this book is written hopefully, with compassion for my white liberal friends, with the conviction that "white liberal" is not a dirty word and that, if anything, we need more of them, and especially with the hope that their efforts, undertaken with greater insight, less hysteria and more humor (which has saved us blacks from despair), can turn white America's racial attitudes around . . . while there is still time and room in which to turn.

# I

# White Racism—Or What To Do Until We Find a Cure for This Madness

For all intents and purposes, white racism is a psychological disease that afflicts a full ninety-eight percent of all Caucasoids living today. It is found in a particularly devastating strain in the United States where the malady has been allowed to develop unchecked for over three hundred years, and in certain parts of the British Isles and the African continent where its sufferers have been brought into prolonged contact with dark-skinned people. Ironically, exhaustive research seems to indicate that people of color are not the carriers of the disease; they merely evoke its manifestation. But when it does appear, it grows rapidly to epidemic proportions, and although there are no reported fatalities that have been caused by it, white racism is known to have an appallingly crippling effect on entire populaces. As yet, there is no known cure.

The symptoms of this disease vary greatly according to geography, age, and the educational and social level of the region. In its milder forms, it is characterized by an uneasiness toward people of color—not necessarily personal contact, it should be noted, but toward black people as a subject rather than an object. Patients in this stage of the illness will frequently venture the observation, "I work with them every day," or "I have a friend who is one," but simultaneously they express mild to deep-seated fears over the prospect of "one" moving into the neighborhood or that "they" will strong-arm an unsuspecting white innocent in the streets. In its more advanced form, the disease is known to give rise to frequent fits of hysteria whenever the subject is mentioned. Advanced stages also show profound sexual fantasies; here the patient will offer observations that "they" are known to be immoral or project fears that "one" is apt to want to marry his daughter. In some areas, such fantasies have led to cases of massive, collective aggressiveness; verified reports exist of white racists who have lynched people of color whom they suspected of even entertaining such thoughts.

Such cases have been somewhat rare in the past few years, although a rash of outbreaks has been documented in the southern United States in the past decade and a particularly bad occurrence was reported in Detroit during the summer of 1967 (now logged in the annals as the Algiers Motel Incident). By far, the most active cases occur in a milder form, but since so little is known about this disease that affects so many and since it reaches epidemic proportions so quickly, observers of this phenomenon are greatly concerned that some cure be found for it as rapidly as possible.

# I

One of the greatest problems in medicine, so the doctors tell us, is getting a person to accept the fact that he is ill, to recognize what caused his illness (whether excessive smoking, overeating, too much or too little exercise) and to take the prescribed cure. If this is a problem for illnesses that are physical in nature, it is compounded enormously when we deal with an emotional disease that most sufferers will not admit having and for which, even if they did, there is no verified cure—no way even of relieving the pain, which the patient doesn't acknowledge having either. So it is with white racism—a problem as old as this nation itself but one which the United States did not accurately identify until an empaneled federal Commission carefully diagnosed the illness and released its findings in the spring of 1968. Ironically, the Commission's Report, which accurately pinpointed the malady, prescribed a cure not for its sufferers but for the black people who, as noted earlier, are not carriers of the disease but merely trigger its outbreaks. In effect, therefore, the Kerner Commission ended up by substantiating the worst fears of white racists. By arguing that blacks must be educated, put in decent homes, taken off welfare rolls, given jobs and valid reasons to trust the police, the Kerner Commission did what it obviously had no intention of doing: giving further credence to the widespread opinion that black people are ignorant, sloppy, lazy and lawless!

In the final analysis, few white people took the Kerner Report seriously, as its own Commission members lamented a year after its release. This was both unfortunate and inevitable —inevitable because the Commission set about its task with two strikes against it, and unfortunate because its findings were so significant. Had the Commission not been, by definition, locked into the necessity of finding a cause and a cure for the riots of the preceding five years, it could have dealt either with white racism or the urban slums—both of which are desperately critical problems in American society. But because it tried to speak to both problems, and in an atmosphere intensively warmed and made hostile by the urban explosions which brought about its creation, the Kerner Report ended up saying nothing—to which a majority of the people it wanted to reach were willing to listen.

Accordingly we are left with the predicament of having had for the first time in American history a definitive assessment of what is wrong with the nation's black-white relations, made by a prestigious federal Commission, and with no one, including the President who established it and his successor, willing to accept the validity of its conclusions. And yet, upon the recognition of that validity hangs whatever substantive efforts the nation will make to eradicate the disease of white racism from its midst.

In retrospect, we can recognize that the term "white racism" itself very quickly began to suffer from what in military circles would be called "overkill." No public report has been released in recent years with the sound and fury that accompanied the issuance of the Kerner Report, and when it was made public, the term quickly became consecrated by the mass media as part of the new American vocabulary. Simultaneously it became a battle cry for the rising tide of black militants (who, it is little known, were rapidly running out of epithets to fling in the teeth of the enemy). Suddenly, like the word "communism" in the McCarthy era, everyone began to see white racism everywhere: in the board room of General Motors and the traffic cop on the corner, in white teachers in black schools and black workers in white factories. Because it rapidly came to describe too much, the term "white racism" may have died aborning by describing nothing. And if this is the case, it is one of the great tragedies of our time, for just as we are discovering what this national affliction is that has troubled our economy, our national character, our ability to be taken seriously as a free and democratic society, and our sense of justice and equality, we are in danger of having the whole white nation turn its back on the diagnosis and thus block the important efforts that must be made to effect a remedy for its cure.

Ironically, this is precisely what seems to be taking place today. The Kerner Report was designed to turn this nation on, to arouse an indifferent and lethargic white America to the real reasons for racial strife and to impel the nation toward its resolution. Instead, it has had the opposite effect; the Report has not even been read by the people who most need to digest it, and the label "white racism" has turned off and been tuned out by an overwhelming number of the people to whom it is directed. We may need therefore a new term, something like substituting "carcinoma" for "cancer," which identifies the same reality but somehow just doesn't sound quite as bad, or at the very least leaves one with the hope that the experts who could create such an efficacious term can also find an effective cure.

However, until and unless this happens, we still have to deal with the reality that is called "white racism," to convince millions of white Americans that they are indeed its victims, and

that the failure to recognize its malignant effects, on thems
as well as on black Americans, will in the long run be termi
. . . for the nation. To do this, it should be noted, takes an extraordinary amount of trust in the redemptive quality of
people in general and white people in particular. The history of
America shows very little evidence of the willingness of white
Americans to do anything in regard to the black issue that they
have not been forced to do either by internal strife or external
threat. This is why the three greatest periods of black progress
in America are co-terminous with the three great wars this
nation has fought: the Civil War which made freedmen out of
slaves, World War I which propelled thousands of blacks from
the South to the North, and World War II which thrust more
thousands of blacks from a life of urban poverty to the thresh-
old of becoming black bourgeoisie. Many black people recognize
this fact of life in American history, and for this very reason
they have no patience with suggestions of long-term therapy;
for them the cancerous tumor of racism is ripe and ready for
quick surgery . . . and they are ready to use meat cleavers if
necessary to cut it out.

For those who still believe there is some therapeutic value in
less drastic measures, there remains the necessity, indeed the
urgency, of getting down to the business of effecting a cure.
Before examining the resources (and problems!) of the therapist,
however, let's look a bit more closely at the patient.

## II

Just what is white racism and who is a white racist? Assum-
ing that bigotry is not dead in American society and that the
racial bigot, apart from some miraculous conversion (which
now and then is known to occur), is beyond hope, white racism
can be identified as a less crass, often more unconscious feeling of racial antipathy or, in many cases, of racial superiority
that affects and afflicts white people. Its insidiousness lies
primarily in the fact that it is so often unconscious: it is manifest in people who would never think of themselves as racial

...arned to spell and pronounce Negro without
...," who have long since gotten over saying
...ames in addressing black people they don't
...be so familiar with, and who don't lose
...ck person is seated at the next table in a
...cy may even be persons who work side by side
...sk by desk with black people, who ride to the office on the
same bus and shop in the same stores, and who may indeed
live in the same neighborhood (loosely defined) with black citizens. But somehow they just cannot shake loose the feeling that
there *is* a difference! Of course they recognize that all blacks
are not on ADC and that some blacks do keep up their neighborhoods and that some are as intelligent as any white man
(especially if the "some" is Ralph Bunche or Thurgood Mar-
shall). But the difference is still there, and as a last resort the
white racist takes comfort in the fact that most black people
recognize the difference also, for "they" too will tell you that
"they" prefer to be with "their own kind."

In addition there is the problem of all these riots and crime
in the streets and declining property values when "they" move
in. And even the most enlightened of white racists have problems in coming to terms with these situations. It is to no avail
to point out that the riots—whether campus or urban—have
not been exclusively black affairs, or that every criminal the
police arrest is not black, or that property values do not decline
when a black family moves in . . . unless a sizable number of
white families panic and flood the market with homes for sale.
The white racist remains virtually unconvinced. He begins with
his general ignorance (or, more politely, his lack of awareness)
of matters racial, which is compounded by his latent prejudice,
reinforced by the mass media, and confirmed by every wild
story that his neighbors and relatives repeat. Moving him off
of dead center is a monumental task.

White racism also affects institutions as well as individuals,
and perhaps more devastatingly in the long run. Until a few
years ago, individual bigotry was out of vogue, at least in the
North and especially among the more intelligent, whether in
labor unions or banking circles. But it is frightfully easier to

conceal racist attitudes in institutional policies and processes than it is to reflect them in one's personal practices. The most liberal-minded union leader can still take refuge behind seniority rules, personnel managers who are racially "with it" can still rely on pre-employment tests, and civic-conscious bankers can still depend upon credit ratings to determine—objectively, so it is said—how the ball game will be played, by whom, for how long, where, and by whose rules.

Perhaps the key word in this analysis is "unconscious." The white racist is not a loud-mouthed bigot or a staunch segregationist. He is for fair play and equal opportunity and justice for all, but he is also out to protect his own interests, to look out for his own family and to preserve his own way of life, and whatever from his perspective may threaten those sacred priorities is to him dangerous. It simply compounds the danger if the threat comes from quarters composed of people who, after all, are different!

In essence, therefore, what we encounter in confronting the white racist is a basically decent but very frightened person who feels threatened by all that surrounds him. The old alma mater that he remembers or is sending his kids to has become the private preserve of militants and radicals, the old neighborhood has gone to pot (figuratively in some instances, narcotically in others), the shop is hiring ex-cons or the boss wants him to have a black secretary, taxes are up, crime is on a rampage and the latest move-in was only twenty-two blocks away! And when his liberal priest or do-good pastor calls *him* a racist, that is adding insult to injury.

To describe the harborer of these fears as a frightened person (perhaps even a frightened, *little* person) is not to speak disparagingly, but to describe honestly the way millions of white Americans feel. They are little persons in an immensely big and complex world which makes them feel smaller every day—what with big business and big government dominating the scene, and machines and computers replacing skilled and unskilled alike. And they are frightened—or perhaps "anxious" is the more accurate word. All the things they've believed in and striven for and looked to seem to be crumbling around their ears. Nothing—not even the Catholic Church—seems content with the way things are; everyone wants everything changed, from the draft laws to the Latin Mass. Consequently it's easiest (and most reassuring) to resist change from those sectors which demand the loudest, threaten the most and seem to offer the least. And this, in brief, is why we are plagued with the disease of white racism. The frightened (little) white American has convinced himself that by capitulating to racial demands he has the least to gain and the most to lose . . . and he doesn't intend to lose graciously or willingly.

To penetrate this fog of fear, therefore, we would do well to recognize that when we deal with white racism, we are dealing with basically frightened people who should be approached more with compassion than with bombast. And we would do well also to appeal to their own self-interests rather than to profound moralisms about justice and equality (to which most Americans only give lip service anyway). When it comes to confronting the suburban white mentality, as we shall see later, the self-interest approach is particularly difficult, but in the long run it is as effective as anything we know. For too long in American society we have tried to effect change by appeals to moral instincts and humanitarian principles—and they simply don't work. But tell white America that its racial illness is costing it money—that the white racist is paying more taxes and getting less for them, that he is losing money every time he sells his home to get away from "them," and that the welter of suburban enclaves he has created in the last two decades as the last bastion of defense against the advancing black hordes are vulnerable—and perhaps then he will listen. If not, the illness can be then defined as terminal and we can simply await expiration . . . only the disease will carry off not only the victim but his way of life along with him.

It is admittedly shock therapy that is called for in this most critical and unusual of diseases, but a therapy (let my black brothers note) far more effective, potentially, than those superstitious, witchcraft-like methods advocated in some black circles where exorcism of the evil spirit by threat of fire is advocated. (This treatment is also advocated by a few white practitioners also, but like most witch doctors they can be dismissed as frauds.) Shock therapy however is an exceedingly delicate and difficult treatment to use in any situation; as we shall see, as much depends on the skill of the therapist as on the therapy itself. And for the record, let it be noted that there are very few therapists these days who are competent to deal with white racism.

# II

# To Be Or Not To Be ...
# A White Liberal

The decline and fall of the white liberal in America is one of the more amusing chapters of American history. Never found in large numbers, he nevertheless compensated for his small ranks by the enormous fervor with which he gave himself to his causes. Whether championing the issue of anti-slavery or defending the rights of organized labor or decrying the brutal side-effects of 19th-century industrialism and 20th-century corruption in city politics, the white liberal has fought his battles with conviction and perseverance . . . and, surprisingly, won a few skirmishes here and there. On the racial issue in American society, however, the white liberal has, since the turn of the present century, been passing through increasingly progressive stages of confusion and indecision, so that currrently he finds himself on the brink of despair.

I

The chief dilemma of the white liberal on race has been a growing lack of clarity about the goals of the racial revolution —a lack that has increased with each successive escalation of the conflict. When, for example, the bulk of black people in American society were held as slaves, the goal of the white liberal was crystal-clear: he could and did crusade for their emancipation. Once they were freed, his task was equally clear (although not as enlightened): they must be educated. Accordingly, thousands of white liberals swarmed into the South setting up schools and universities, teaching the freed slaves skills in agriculture and trades and guiding their entry into Southern politics. (Unfortunately, white liberals were preparing blacks for a way of life that was already on the wane; unfortunately, also, today's militant blacks have had to erect a statue of Uncle Tom over the remains of Booker T. Washington for giving aid and comfort to this process.)

With the advent of World War I, however, and the migration to the North of thousands of black Southerners who had by now discovered that the agricultural South held no promise for them, white liberals began to have second thoughts about the entire matter. On the one hand, the new black immigrants did solve the northern problem of the shortage in unskilled labor brought about by the Congressional repression of European immigration in the 1920's. But on the other hand, the problem was no longer one which was confined to a backward, ignorant and inhumane South; white liberals literally now had to live with their liberalism, and for liberals of any sort, this is always most difficult to do!

And so, white liberalism (which until recent years was the only known antidote for white racism, but a remedy peculiar to the northern regions of the United States), confronted by the disease on its own doorsteps, took refuge in that most popular device of social change in America—a committee. The deeper the crisis became, the more the committees that were established, all committed ostensibly to the same cause, all competing desperately for the same funds, and all entrenching themselves professionally and semi-permanently in the racial fray. Indeed, race relations (as it was curiously then called) began to develop into a growing business of sorts; by the decade of the 50's (and amply spurred on by a few World War II riots) interrracial committees were becoming municipal commissions, every religious denomination had its social action committee prodding local churches to get into the act, and a national association of intergroup relations people was holding annual conventions in which the pros always managed to pass a yearly resolution demanding higher professional standards for participation in this newly emerging guild.

While committees were thus forming—and reforming—(themselves) and passing resolutions and pleading for larger budgets, the Depression, and the War which followed, moved the nation's black populace a halting step forward on its quest for decency and justice. The reforms of the New Deal era, because they were aimed at improving the lot of the poor, had a profound impact on the status of thirteen million black people. But the Second World War did what nothing else could have done; it desegregated the U.S. Armed Forces, broke down employment discrimination in factories, gave blacks the same wages as whites and set the social climate for the two landmark, post-war decisions on race by the U.S. Supreme Court: the restrictive covenant decision of 1948 which for the first time broke open the housing market in the North, and the Brown vs. Topeka decision of 1954 which, at least in theory, broke the back of school segregation in the South.

White liberals took both great pride and undue credit for these developments. (It is difficult to find a white liberal today who was not personally involved, to hear him tell it, in winning these great blows for justice and equality.) The racial millennium seemed just around the corner, and black citizens were assured that, given a few more generations of waiting for these new developments to take effect, their entry into American society would be accomplished (if not for their grandchildren, then certainly for their great-grandchildren).

For some strange and still unexplainable reason, however, the supposedly grateful black populace decided that they didn't really care to wait that long! In December, 1955 a quiet, modest black seamstress in Montgomery, Alabama decided she couldn't wait for her great-grandchildren to get seats on public busses, a few years later black college students decided they couldn't wait in the hope that their posterity could eat hot dogs at a dime store lunch counter, and by the mid-sixties Northern blacks were becoming angrily convinced that they were not going to wait for another three or four or five generations to have a chance for a decent home, a steady job and a good education for their children. Martin Luther King, Jr. eloquently spelled all of this out for white America, telling the nation *Why We Can't Wait* . . . but his words fell on deaf ears. White liberals nevertheless persisted in the belief that, given time and persistent prodding, the twin-headed monster of discrimination and bigotry would be slain, once and for all.

But black people were beginning to press for a different timetable, dramatically caught up in those two, blunt, weary-of-waiting words "Freedom Now!" And in fairness to white liberals, it must be said that most of them were willing to strategically shift their time perspectives to accommodate this new black mood, although many grumbled privately that it was moving too far, too fast. Yet, when they went to Birmingham and Selma and saw the impact those encounters appeared to have on the national, white conscience, they also began to shift their social philosophies. King had given not only his people but white liberalism in America a new strategy based upon a new philosophy of social change, and white liberals found themselves for the first time following the time schedule, the tactics and the philosophy of black leadership. It necessitated a radical readjustment for the white liberal perspective, but it was, after all, a philosophy as peaceful as the teachings of Jesus and a tactic hallowed by the great, white apostle of passive resistance, Henry Thoreau. White liberalism therefore bought it with growing enthusiasm and without many misgivings.

The problem was that the blacks who bought it also were primarily Southern; those in the North who became enamored with the King philosophy were mainly the black bourgeoisie—who already had it made. But in the slightly amended words of Holy Writ, "there arose some black Pharaohs who knew not this new Moses"—black leadership of different perspectives and persuasions who had little regard for the King philosophy and less for his strategy. Impatient with the attempts to catch white America's ear, they determined to catch its eye; if white people would not listen, they would certainly have to look . . . while angry blacks set about burning the cities of the nation to ashes.

It is here that the confusion and despair of white liberalism set in. Their timetable drastically altered but their hopes renewed by the advent of the King movement, white liberals responded with shock and amazement to the billowing clouds of smoke that began to arise, summer after summer, over the major cities of America. They watched anxiously for signs that would indicate whether the loyalties of the nation's black people were shifting . . . and where—from King to Carmichael, from Young to Brown? And finally, with the murder of King, their hopes were dashed completely. The great apostle of non-violence had died by a violent act, and with him, it was feared, died any hope of containing or channeling the growing rage of black Americans.

The white liberal response to this crisis was one of pathos. Many threw up their hands in horror and disgust; if the new mood was to be one of rampant militancy, they wanted no part of it (which, of course, cast some doubts on their racial convictions in the first place). Others, with equally doubtful sincerity, began to rush headlong into the militant camp, issuing solemn pronouncements designed to rationalize or, even worse, enshrine violence as a new dogma in the American creed, and pouring money into the hands of every black, newly ordained (and often self-appointed) leader who threatened bigger and better fires if his demands were not met. For the most part, however, white liberals simply suffered a paralysis of nerve. Not knowing to what or to whom to turn, they opted for retreat, in order to await a fresh signal to regroup their decimated forces.

## II

Consequently, the white leadership to whom the nation must look to rally the white troops for a new assault on the bastion of racism is in sad disarray—lacking aim, direction and leadership. Those few white guerrillas who have not forsaken the battlefield have by and large traded skillful strategy for storm-trooper tactics. Now that the scene of battle has shifted from carefully calculated, well-coordinated attacks on citadels of institutionalized discrimination (Congress, business, etc.) to the new battle plan focused on a new enemy and drawn up by the Kerner Commission, there is a small but vociferous white contingent prepared to make the same mistake of some of their black counterparts . . . to harangue the enemy to death. What persuasion won't achieve, they hope pompous bombast will, and so they write off white racists as hopeless causes and denounce them as unredeemable relics of a racist culture.

Given these polarities of rising black militancy and cynical white radicalism, the great majority of America's white racists have nowhere to turn. Despised and rejected on the one hand, courted and curried by semi-respectable brands of outright white bigotry on the other, the nation's white racists are like frightened sheep without skillful shepherds who are willing to steer a firm, progressive course between bigotry and tyranny. And yet—potentially, at least—if their racist attitudes can be changed and their racial hang-ups overcome, today's white racists might become that sector of American society which will positively determine the outcome of the racial struggle in this nation.

Realistically, it is this sector that will make the difference either way—positively or negatively—simply because, in this democratic society, their sentiments will sway the future (a fact well recognized in the last presidential election). And because they are not only the majority but a frightened one on matters of race, the danger is enormously great that their racist sentiments will become translated into repressive policies, both public and private. Frightened people are ripe targets for demagogues and tyrants; with appalling rapidity they can slip into the posture of a well-dressed, well-spoken, white liberal, female type who recently remarked to me: "Maybe the trouble with this nation is that we have too much democracy!" If such a sentiment ever really takes root in the minds of the white majority, we can all throw in the towel—militants, moderates, cynics, radicals and revolutionaries alike.

And so, we find ourselves with the urgent need to resurrect the best features of white liberalism but also to refashion a new kind of white liberal, one who is considerably more enlightened, less likely to freeze or panic when the battle gets rough, and more committed to the painful process of dealing with white racism than of trying to determine the fate and direction of black militancy. White liberals, in essence, need to doff their battle fatigues and don the attire of practitioners in the skilled art of probing white racist minds, finding out what makes them tick and how they can be mentally recycled to become truly decent and humane persons.

This brings us momentarily back to the business of shock therapy. We will return to the techniques of this approach in a later chapter; for the present let's content ourselves with a brief discourse on its dangers. One does not need even a marginal knowledge of the techniques of shock therapy in psychiatry to recognize that it is not one hundred percent effective, that it can produce side-effects as damaging as the psychosis it is designed to cure, and (what is most obvious) that an overdose can be fatal. (Indeed, not without a touch of irony, one notes that the same technique which can be used for treating mental illness is used, in stronger dosage, for executing criminals!) Let this therefore be the first warning to our new breed of shock therapists in dealing with the mental aberrations of white racism. Since we propose to recruit this new cadre from the decimated ranks of white liberalism, it should be borne in mind that liberalism, with its emphasis historically on the rights of the individual, inevitably produces two side-effects: the first is a conservative reaction, and the second is a moral dilemma to which modern liberalism is especially vulnerable. The first danger is a calculated risk: how to produce enough movement and sufficient change that will be counted as valid by the minority without triggering a hostile, repressive response from the majority. There are no hard-and-fast rules on this one, except to fly by the seat of one's trousers (with the added note that the trousers should be those of a sensitive social observer and not the overalls of the foreman of a wrecking crew)!

The second problem is the more difficult because of its subtlety and because of the half-truth it contains. White liberalism, with its fundamental faith in and regard for the rights of the individual, stands accused today in American society of ignoring precisely those rights when it comes to the expressed opinions, values and wishes of the average (frightened) white

American. "The do-gooders are trying to cram this race business down our throats" cries the beleaguered white racist. "No one is concerned about the policeman's rights anymore" bemoan the fraternal societies of police officers (and, incidentally, one of the most powerful political forces in American urban society today). "What about my rights" shrieks the suspicious white homeowner, and in chorus they all chant: "With all this fuss about Negro rights, doesn't the white man have any rights anymore?"

Honesty compels us to admit that they have a point . . . of sorts, but beyond saying this, it is difficult to determine precisely what the point is. If the complaint is that white privileges are being curtailed so that black rights can be enjoyed, painful as it may be for the whites, there is really no alternative. White privileges in this nation have, as a matter of fact, been enjoyed at the expense of black, constitutional—not to mention moral—rights for centuries. Consequently, if setting the record straight means giving up special privileges so that everyone can partake of constitutional rights (i.e., little things like voting and living where you wish and can afford and being free of intimidation and harassment), then that is the price white America will have to pay . . . and the bill is three hundred years overdue! On the other hand, if white rights (e.g., policemen's rights, homeowners' rights, etc.) are merely ill-disguised and arrogant excuses for wanting the freedom to be a bigot or a segregationist *and* have the protection of the state—its laws, customs and institutions—while doing so, then we have to point out that, although it may not be fully recognized, that sort of business went out with kerosene lamps!

Nevertheless, the liberal's dilemma at this point is a real one; if he clings to the sacredness of individual rights, he must somehow convince his racist antagonist that the latter's rights are not to be confused with special privileges which he may have unconsciously enjoyed without realizing that he did so at someone else's expense. Simultaneously, he must guard against the possibility of exchanging one injustice for another—of feeling so guilty over three hundred years of white injustice that he is willing to exchange it for an indeterminate period of black tyranny. (Note: black tyrants are proportionately much smaller than their white counterparts, but, believe it or not, they do exist.)

In employing shock treatment, therefore, the therapist will have to watch out that he does not become hoisted on his own petard, or, therapeutically speaking, that he doesn't find himself strapped to the same treatment table on which he is trying so desperately to pin down his patient. He cannot, of course, turn off his patient's protestations about white rights with sublime rejoinders about white duties and responsibilities (although this is his patient's favorite reply whenever black rights are raised in discussion). Nor can he scrap the whole notion of individual rights—white or black—as an outmoded philosophical and political creed; for all its difficulties, especially in an age in which independence and individualism are hard to come by, there is still some virtue in the notion that every man should determine his own destiny.

What the therapist can do—and finally we come to the essence of our shock therapy approach, the principle on which the whole treatment rests—is to encourage his patient to believe—to convince his racist sufferer of the notion—that the idea of racial separatism (with some slight modifications, of course) is back in vogue, that he doesn't need to feel guilty about "them" wanting to be with their own kind, and that as long as he does nothing overtly to push black thought more rapidly in this direction, he stands a good chance that black people may come out thinking pretty much as he does! When the racist hears this, he may just sigh in relief and forget the whole messy business, or he may become so incensed that "they" are becoming like him that he will pompously move to an integrationist stance, just to maintain that all-important difference. Or he may collapse and die of shock! Either alternative would be a considerable improvement over the present chaotic situation.

# III

# Diagnosing the Disease

A significant amount of the sophistication and effectiveness of civil rights strategy disappeared with the discovery of white racism. Before black men found out that the malady from which white men suffered stemmed from a single and frightfully common virus, they fought the disease of bigotry and prejudice on the mistaken notion that its origins were as varied as its symptoms. For over fifty years dedicated black men and women, together with a small band of white supporters, pursued a battle on many fronts to rid the nation of the plague of racial prejudice. They mounted an assault in the courts and legislatures to get laws passed or interpreted that would control its spread. They pressured American business, industry and labor to thwart its practice. In Little Rock, Birmingham and Selma they mounted vast public campaigns with the aid of the mass media to expose the tragedy of hapless whites caught in terminal stages of the dread disease. Finally, through an ever increasing array of volunteer organizations, the foes of bigotry launched a nationwide educational blitz designed to warn the American people of the dangers of this illness, and especially to inoculate the young who it was assumed were relatively under-exposed to the disease and who hopefully, through the curative powers of education, could be protected from its devastating results.

The discovery that it is really racism which has caused the whole mess, however, has momentarily thrown black people for a loop. Identifying racism as the source of the problem— the virus that gives rise to bigotry and prejudice—is in itself a significant breakthrough; at least we now know what we're fighting! But identifying the virus has not as yet led to the discovery of a vaccine that will effect a cure, and herein lies the dilemma. As long as black people thought the problem was one of ignorance or obstinacy, they could readily apply the twin compresses of education and legislation. But when the problem was finally diagnosed as basically congenital (i.e., peculiar to the white species) with profound psychological overtones, blacks were left without a remedy. Some quickly sensed that, in the absence of a cure, it would be temporarily effective to engage in prolonged descriptions of the disease, usually in its most deadly form. Others decided that finding a cure for racism is as hopeless as discovering a remedy for the common cold, and have accordingly given up the battle as a lost cause. Still others, appalled by the effect that racism has had on its white victims, have moved with dispatch to isolate and insulate the black populace from its terrible effects. But in most segments of the black community today there is the common conviction that we are no longer dealing with a malignant tumor in the nation's life which can be deftly removed by laws and education; we confront instead a virus which must be wiped out before it destroys all of us—black and white alike.

The most vocal, and thereby the most widely known, exponents on the subject of wiping out white racism have managed to combine and popularize a two-pronged treatment-approach: a constant harangue of the patient on how vile is the disease with which he is afflicted, and the continual threat to dispose of the patient if he doesn't get better. This is where sophistication has been lost in treatment and where a less dramatic but more clinical approach might yield far greater effectiveness.

We might begin, for example, with an attempt to identify certain types of white racism or categories of white racists. A particularly recent and subtle strain has been discovered on American college and university campuses and appears to be directly associated with the scholarly mentality (hence its identification as *mens genus scholasticus*). This breed of scholarly racism emerged with the reluctant recognition that research on the sex life of the Samoans or Pidgin English in the Malay Peninsula had been fairly well worked over, and the simultaneous discovery that a fertile research field on the same themes of sex and dialect lies literally in the black backyards of most academic campuses. As a consequence, by examining with clinical precision the strange, new world of black culture, a host of bright, young and courageous white intellectuals have carved out academically prestigious and financially rewarding niches for themselves. For the most part, they engage (as an Oxford student is alleged to have said about his tutor) in "profound and mysterious probings of the obvious," but they find their work eagerly sought by commercial publishers (who in turn have recently discovered that black titles make best sellers) and their insights readily marketable to governmental commissions (who languish in the mistaken belief that as long as the nation studies the black problem, it won't have to do anything about it).

Scholarly research on black America has caused some dire misgivings in academic circles, especially among those intellectuals whose esoteric disciplines do not readily provide a rationale for their getting into the act. As a result, on the campuses these days one hears anxious mutterings about the extent to which the problems of black Americans (usually concealed under such scholarly euphemisms as "the urban crisis" or "social dynamics of the disadvantaged") are creeping more and more into the curricula and budgets of our nation's ivory towers. Those academicians who are anxious about this trend can put their minds to rest, however. Scholarly objectivity (which means: Never get personally involved in anything that captures your intellectual interest) still prevails among white academic experts on black folk. Besides, most black folk are street-wise to the research game and have devised a community pact to give researchers (most of whom are graduate students anxious to carve out *their* turf on this vast, uncharted landscape of black studies) all the wrong answers (which is why the contradictory findings of an overwhelming commitment to integration and a growing belief in black separatism keeps cropping up in research studies).

Scholarly racism, however, affects a relatively small portion of the nation's populace and policies. Far more influential, and therefore more dangerous, is the racism that appears peculiar to practitioners in the mass media: journalists, radio and TV announcers and commentators, editorial writers, movie makers, and the like. At the outset, it should be noted that success in this burgeoning industry demands an omnicompetence in all subjects, or at least the willingness to think that one is omniscient. This basic factor, combined with the enormous influence of the American communications industry whose nationwide depictions of Birmingham's Bull Connor and Selma's Sheriff Clark undoubtedly contributed to a national reassessment of the necessity of federal civil rights legislation, has given rise to a somewhat exaggerated positive self-image which the mass media has of itself on matters racial.

The media mentality, which is by and large a product of the North, performed admirably as long as it was exposing the barbarism, decadence and stupidity of racism in the South. But when the scene shifted from Birmingham to Buffalo and from Philadelphia, Mississippi to Philadelphia, Pennsylvania, suddenly the antics of a Sheriff Rainey became overshadowed by the looters in Harlem, Hough and Detroit. Those sensitive interpreters of the life-style of the South either forgot or, what is more likely, never realized that the South they so righteously condemned produced many of the conditions and people they managed to distort in the North. They overlooked also the racism of their own Northern communities—the poverty, the slums, the disease, the unemployment—which makes the difference between the South and the North one of degree, not of kind. Black people discovered in the process that TV camera lenses work exceptionally well at long range, but cloud the picture fantastically on closeups.

However, the myopic racism of the mass media is only shared, after all, by a vast segment of white America that suffers from the devastating effects of the Horatio Alger strain of this disease. The easiest to diagnose and the most common variety of the virus, the Horatio Alger strain has been developed from that common experience of most white Americans whose forebears came to these shores in generations past, plugged into the Protestant ethic (i.e., they worked hard, lived frugally, saved their money and prayed on Sunday) and, in one or two generations, became instant American success stories. This brand of racism is quickly identifiable by such sincere but self-righteous comments as, "My parents or my family worked hard to get where we are. No one gave anything to us. If these blacks want equality, why don't they work for it the same way we had to?"

It may be true that, with the exception of those aristocrats whose wealth, jobs, and family status are an accident of genes, most Americans have had to work hard for whatever they have. But no segment of the American populace has had to work at being equal . . . except, of course, the nation's black people. Somehow in that peculiar mentality reserved for white America, it has been given to black Americans to "prove" themselves, to demonstrate in advance their worthiness of being treated like human beings. And this is made the more ironic by the fact that black Americans were the one segment of the nation who for two hundred years were systematically stripped of any vestige of humanness. They were sold like cattle, forbidden to learn to read and write, denied any semblance of family life, bred like mink when their diminishing numbers were needed to survive an expanding cotton economy, finally emancipated after their continued servitude had plunged the nation into war and there seemed, in Lincoln's words, no other way to "preserve the Union"—and then told, for the next one hundred years, to prove themselves equal.

If the unmitigated gall that characterizes this position is not apparent, then perhaps the practical realities will be, and while they are ancient history perhaps, for the record they bear repeating. Most white Americans worked their way to the top when there was still a vast supply of unskilled jobs available in this nation. The white workers, mainly immigrants, who manned the mills and factories from the 1880's to the 1930's also produced the sons who went to college, entered the professions and helped to create the new technology which, among other things, made unskilled labor a useless commodity. Black workers did not get into business and industry in any signifi-

cant numbers until after the Depression, just a generation before business and industry began to discover it could turn out
its products more cheaply and efficiently (i.e., with less labor
problems) by using machines instead of men. Therefore, in today's automated, technological society, telling an unskilled
black worker with a 5th grade education to work his way to
the top is about as crass as telling a kid in the Soap Box
Derby that he has the privilege of competing in the Indian-
apolis 500.

An additional fact of life also often escapes the memories of
the millions of America's mini-Horatio Algers. When the
Irish in 19th-century Boston saw signs saying "No Irish need
apply," they could go home and practice losing their brogue.
Polish Americans could drop the "ski" from their names (and
many did), Italians could learn to cook with less garlic, and
Jewish Americans could manage to deftly conceal the Yiddish
News behind the New York Times. But the possibility of
black Americans concealing their blackness, except by generations of race-mixing, is the ultimate in impossibility. A few
white visionaries have been brash enough to suggest such an
option for resolving America's racial dilemma, but few black
persons have ever taken the suggestion seriously, a fact for which
most white people have been profoundly grateful.

In fact, today the tables are turned, and all those white racists who have lived in fear that the hearts of their daughters
would be captured by a black suitor ought to rejoice greatly in
this new turn of events. Black is now in vogue among black folk;
it is no longer something to be concealed beneath good gram-
mar and a college degree. Instead it is an essence to be revealed in pride, with all its accompanying accoutrements:
African dress and hairstyles, soul food diets, special hand-
shakes of greeting reserved for the soul brother and, among the
elite, a few words of Swahili thrown in the conversation for
good measure. One would think that white racists, especially
the Horatio Alger variety, would find considerable relief in
this development. Black pride is in a curious sense taking the
Alger advocates at their word. Black people are increasingly
turning their attention inward to their own communities,

learning their own history, developing their own economic and cultural institutions, searching for their own identity, and becoming increasingly determined to shape their own destinies. It is a lesson, after all, which blacks have learned from white America: the Poles, the Irish, the Italians, the Slavs, the Roman Catholic Church, the Protestant establishment and the Jewish community (and every other identifiable white segment of America), all of whom managed to combine their struggle to make it in the mainstream of America with the development of strong, viable and internal political-economic structures.

But when this development is pointed out to the whites who cling to the Horatio Alger mythology, they still remain unhappy. Polish factory workers, busily unwrapping their kielbasa at lunch time, still can't understand all this talk about soul food. Americans with the most remote drop of Irish blood in their veins, who couldn't speak two words of Gaelic if their lives depended on it, drape (and douse) themselves on St. Patrick's Day with anything green they can lay their hands on, but simultaneously get "up-tight" if they see a black man wearing an African-style shirt. Jewish Zionists who fervently support the state of Israel become semi-hysterical when they hear talk of establishing a separate black nation in the southern United States.

In essence, when blacks preached integration, whites heard intermarriage; when blacks talk separatism, whites see disloyalty. Blacks therefore may have to move to a double-pronged assault and tackle this brand of white racism from both vantage points by preaching separatism and practicing intermarriage. Caught between the prospects of these twin disasters, white America might resign itself to the only other alternative, painful though the thought of it may be: to make the United States a free and just society. And believe it or not, that development would take the wind right out of the sails of the black revolution in America!

Until this utopia comes about, if ever it does, someone should be giving attention to perfecting a vaccine for controlling the virus of white racism at the same time that efforts are being waged to cure its victims. For in this nation we are in the uncomfortable dilemma of having created a society which would produce a whole new generation of white racists in the 1980's, even if by some act of God (which it would probably take) the present generation could be cured overnight. Just as we have learned that a polluted water system can infect an entire community, we ought to realize that polluted policies in Congress, or in city hall or the board rooms of banks or police departments or suburban homeowner groups, carry the deadly virus of racism as swiftly and as effectively as a women's bridge club carries gossip.

Once the need is recognized, however, some brave souls will have to begin the thankless task of experimentation with and perfection of an anti-racism vaccine. They can undoubtedly expect to be greeted with the same abuse and rejection with which Edward Jenner was confronted when he developed a vaccine against smallpox. But his efforts, and those of medical scientists who have followed in his steps, have saved the lives of millions, so perhaps we can learn from their work. (Oddly enough, today there are less vaccines for use with humans than there are with animals, who, it should be noted, are remarkably free from the diseases of war, greed, exploitation and racism. Perhaps, therefore, the rat psychologists are on the right track after all, or, better still, it might be that we need to require all behavioral scientists to study animals exclusively for the next decade in the hope that we humans can learn something of value from their non-human behavior.)

While this decade of research is in process (allowing six months for the behaviorists to draft the proposal, two and one-half years for the federal government to fund it, three years for the actual research, an additional year to draft the findings, and the final three years for some journalist to put the report in intelligible English), we can look to the veterinarians, who have obviously had more success in such matters than medical doctors, to work on an effective vaccine. They will quickly point out that there are three general ways of making a vaccine, once the virus has been identified. The first method calls for using a weakened strain of the disease germ that, in turn, causes the formation of antibodies which fight against the virus. This method of injecting a mild racist into a group of healthy, racist-free whites might prove effective if a sufficient number of non-racist whites could be found. But it would not resolve the problem of inoculating those already affected, a stage of the disease when perhaps inoculation is too late in the first place.

There may however be some merit in at least trying to curb the disease in victims already infected by using the second method (if one does not take the matter too literally)—that of inducing dead germs into the patient. Here the approach would be to inject a racist who has had the disease, and somehow been cured of it, into the poker games, the beauty salon rituals, the cocktail parties, and the board meetings of a body of active racists. The hope is that a cured racist, who still looks and talks and acts as though he ought to be a live case but really isn't, might have such a confusing effect upon the active cases that, in their frustration to convince him that he ought to be as sick as they are, the active racists might cure themselves with the lunacy of their own arguments. (Actually, there is just such a case on record, personally observed by the author, in which an active racist, in the advanced stage of the disease, set out to prove to a white companion that the black revolution was in reality an ill-concealed attempt on the part of black men to marry white women. His entire argument crumbled when he suddenly realized that "it takes two to tango"; obviously, from his perspective, the black struggle would collapse if there were no white women willing to marry black men. The latter prospect troubled him deeply, however, and although he is now a cured racist he has become a pronounced anti-feminist.)

The third method, and probably the most reliable, is to pursue the quest of a vaccine that will fight the poisons created by the virus of racism rather than attempting to cure racism itself. It is admittedly a shorter-range solution, although most black people would gladly settle for it. In effect, this method would allow white racists to be as sick as they wish, as long as they do not permit their illness to affect their judgment or their actions. In a sense, developing an anti-toxin approach would represent a continuation, hopefully escalated, of past efforts on the part of black people to deal with white racial hang-ups—only this time black America will learn from its past mistakes. It will not be so sanguine about education as a cure for white racism; while black people were busily educating themselves to enter the white world, it appears they might have done better to educate white folks to enter the human race. Nor will they depend on government and the political process at the federal level to pursue vigorously the cause of finding a cure for the nation's most crippling disease. The Washington establishment, busily arming the nation with thermonuclear hypodermic needles, is far more concerned with some foreign plague (now officially identified as the Red —and, more recently, the Yellow—Peril) than it is with the internal sickness that grips vast segments of the entire populace. Most of all, black America will not place all of its hopes on integration as the answer for our national ills. We pursued that false hope for half a century, and while every quest for a cure can potentially lead one up blind alleys, no one in his wildest moments ever thought that integration would lead to such a dead end.

# IV

# Integration . . . Or the
# Death of an Idea

On March 2, 1969, exactly one year after issuing the report on their momentous discovery of the disease which has caused America's racial suffering for three hundred years, the same team of skilled researchers made the sad, public announcement that one of the valiant warriors in the struggle for racial justice had finally succumbed to its ravaging effects, after a courageous battle against the dread disease over a period of half a century. In somber, clinical tones, the Kerner Commission announced that one of the last, great hopes of modern America, the well-known, highly revered symbol of equality in the nation, N. T. Gration, had passed away in virtual obscurity.

Actually the death notice was slightly ambiguous, as death notices go. In fact, the Kerner team never quite got around to saying that the old stalwart was really dead; they simply lamented the fact that for the preceding twelve months his condition had not improved but instead had deteriorated considerably. But the medical bulletin of a year earlier described N. T. Gration's condition in such hopeless, terminal language that one would be forced to conclude, if he hadn't improved considerably in a year's time, that he had to expire whether his doctors knew it or not.

Oddly enough, the news has not produced any national mourning. A few passionate devotees still refuse to believe that their symbol has perished; they can still be seen driving through the streets of American cities with "God Is Alive" stickers on one side of their rear car bumpers and "One America" (in black and white) on the other. However, most serious minds find it difficult to believe that the question of the Almighty's existence can be confirmed (or denied) by bumper stickers. There is equal reason to doubt that mobile, outdoor advertising accurately reflects the state of the nation's commitment to an ideal about which (much like the Almighty) there is some question as to whether it was ever taken seriously in the first place.

In fact, for the most part, it has been business as usual in America since the passing of N. T. Gration. Some ardent supporters have muttered repeatedly about the violence of the past five years which speeded the demise; others consider his passing the removal of a major roadblock to the acceptance by black people of new leadership (among whom a Rev. O. Lution seems to be gaining increasing popularity, especially among the young). The career of the late N. T. Gration, brief and stormy though it was, is a classic case study of the effects of racism and sheds invaluable light on the course of the disease and its impact on its victims in American society.

# I

N. T. Gration was a child of the twentieth century, but he was also a half-breed and a foreigner; perhaps in those two latter facts more than anything else lies the reason for his miserable life and tragic end. He was sired shortly after the turn of the century by a parentage that was white and liberal on one side, black, angry and hopeful on the other. He was in essence the product of intermarriage (or miscegenation, as the Southerners prefer to call it), and intermarriage has never been a popular idea in America. He came to life in June, 1905 in Niagara Falls, Ontario,* and was born in Canada because there was no room for him in the segregated inns and hotels of America. N. T. Gration began his life, therefore, in the face of almost insurmountable odds; he was the offspring of

*Date of the founding of the Niagara Movement, forerunner of the N.A.A.C.P.

race-mixing, as uncomfortable an idea for white Northerners as it is abhorrent to white Southerners. Only the bleakest of futures could have been predicted for him, even at that early stage in his career.

Quite early in life also, his white parent deserted him, for all practical purposes. The reasons for the desertion are still clouded in obscurity; the mixed marriage may have been too embarrassing, an increasing incompatibility might have developed, or the war, the Roaring Twenties and the Great Depression might have preoccupied his fair-skinned progenitor with other and greater problems. It was not a complete desertion, mind you; Big White Daddy still sent money regularly to support N. T. Gration's schools and colleges or to help pay the legal fees when his progeny got in trouble with the courts; Big Daddy even turned up on occasion for some festive event in N. T. Gration's life (like the annual Brotherhood Week banquet). But throughout this formative period of our symbol's life, it became increasingly clear to him that his white sire had no real commitment to his future, no fundamental desire to help personally in molding and shaping a decent existence for his offspring. There may not have been a divorce, but the separation was real and its effects just as devastating on the fruit of the union.

Like most children of broken marriages, N. T. Gration determined to go it alone and set out in the twenties to prove, in a sense, to his neglectful parent that he could still live up to the old man's hopes. During this period, N. T. Gration heard the voices of the Marcus Garveys and the Elijah Pooles, warning him that Big Daddy was not to be trusted, that for every forward step he took "the Man" would simply raise the admission fee into white society higher, and that his best bet would be with developing his fortunes among his own people. But simultaneously he found that he could get a job in the factories of the North—and five dollars a day certainly beat the three dollars a week that "Mr. Charlie" paid him in the South. And on this slim thread, N. T. Gration decided that perhaps there was some hope; if he could plug into the Protestant ethic—work hard, save his money, buy a home, send his kids to college—his dream just might come true. Big Daddy, from a distance of course, approved; he continued to send money and continually counseled patience: "After all," as he was frequently inclined to observe, "we were two hundred years creating this problem; we won't solve it overnight."

During the Depression years, N. T. Gration fell on hard times, as did nearly everyone else, and, for a brief period, also into bad company. Having diligently pursued his parents' wishes to obtain an education (about the only area of their agreement, but for vastly different reasons), our hero found himself in the 30's among the company of intellectuals. America's intellectuals during the Depression were as poor as everyone else, only their poverty made them take their own ideologies seriously. (This still ranks as one of the strange phenomena among intellectuals whose dedication to their own rhetoric is inversely proportionate to their income.) In this fascinating world of men and ideas, N. T. Gration found himself ardently wooed by the Marxists, a temptation which he found appealing, if for no other reason than the consistent inattention he received from Big Daddy. It should be noted, of course, that N. T. Gration as an intellectual shared this flirtation with Marxism with a good many white writers, artists, unionists and other down-and-outs of the period to whom the white establishment was not being overly generous either. When the war came, this cadre of dissidents all recanted and regained their lost prestige; only N. T. Gration and his clan (if one may be allowed the expression) would still hear Big Daddy's grumblings, twenty years later, about his wild and youthful fling "with the Commies," which N. T. Gration has come to learn represents the ultimate in evils in Big Daddy's world (with intermarriage following as a very close second).

From Marxism to patriotism our hero then moved, with a blind and naive optimism that if he were willing to lay his life on the line for democracy, perhaps white America might take his insistence on sharing in its benefits seriously. And so he marched off to war, serving valiantly in segregated units in the U.S. Army, cooking meals for officers in the Navy (the only assignment obviously for which he was considered qualified) and being all but invisible (if that's conceivable) in the Air Force and the Marines. He gave "the last full measure of sacrifice" in numbers highly disproportionate to the ratio of his fellow clansmen in the general populace, but again he did so cherishing the hope that war against tyranny abroad might change some thinking at home. He came home, however, to the same old story of slums, segregation and solicitous sermonizing on the virtues of patience. During the war, white America had need of every pair of patriotic hands it could muster—including black ones; after the war, for all practical purposes, it was back to business as usual.

It is perhaps understandable that by this time N. T. Gration's patience was wearing a bit thin. He had followed Big Daddy's counsel from afar to the letter (except for that brief lapse with the old man's archenemy— for which he really couldn't be blamed; after all, all white folks sound alike where black folk are concerned). He had gone to school (inferior though it was), gotten jobs (menial though they were), helped fight the old man's war (albeit in "colored" regiments), only to discover that liberty and equality were white ideas—for white men. A few of N. T. Gration's friends made it—here a political appointment, there an assistant something-or-other in charge of colored affairs. But it became quite clear that at the rate N. T. Gration's dream of full acceptance in American society was being realized, it would be the Second Coming before anything significant happened (provided the Good Lord was duly patient and didn't come too quickly)!

And so a dramatic change in course occurred in the American civil rights struggle—a course correction that can be precisely dated on December 1, 1955. On that day, civil rights strategy, planning and decision-making passed from the hands of the professional blacks into the laps of the determined poor. A little black woman in Montgomery, Alabama, imbued with N. T. Gration's dream but unimpressed with his timetable (and even less so with that of his white, liberal cohorts), took matters into her own hands, and from that day till this, things ain't quite been the same in America.

There was a certain white enchantment with Rosa Parks,

the Montgomery Improvement Association and Martin Luther King. After all, with all their fervor and determination, there was still this almost nostalgic belief in the innate goodness of the white mind and its ultimate capitulation to its own principles, especially in the face of such a pure and noble assault on its prejudices as was the Southern Christian Leadership Conference. Even white liberals found a cause and a technique again which were worthy of their commitment, and to their credit they marched and sat and knelt and waded and rode nonviolently with their black brothers. Some, we must never forget, died in that ennobling and tragic brief period in American history—ennobling because it saw some change and because so many of America's finest stories of commitment to this nation's highest ideals were written in this era, but tragic because it was an almost desperate last attempt to make integration a reality in America . . . and it failed.

It failed because black America thought an appeal to the Christian conscience of this nation would bring it to its senses. And that has proven to be an exaggerated estimate either of the depth of conscience or of the significance of Christianity in American society. For the response of the nation to the nonviolent appeals to heal itself was the outbreak of one of the most violent periods in American history—and not the violence of Detroit or Watts or Harlem or Chicago in the mid-sixties which everyone remembers and decries, but the violence of Birmingham and Selma, Alabama and Philadelphia (literal translation: "the city of brotherly love"), Mississippi, and a dozen other cities of the South in the late fifties and early sixties which everyone so easily forgets.

The significance of Christianity in America is questionable; the impact of racism is not. Black people, especially those enamored with the ideals of N. T. Gration, had tried every technique imaginable to translate his hopes into reality. N. T. Gration had been "ailing" (as we say in the ghetto) ever since the Second World War, but like all close comrades, we hated to believe that he could not rally himself and make a comeback. Nevertheless he succumbed, not in the wake of black violence but in the assault of white violence which greeted the last, valiant attempt to make this nation live up to its own stated ideals that America will perhaps ever witness.

## II

It may not be completely inappropriate, however, to hope for a resurrection, or (if that terminology appears too blasphemous) at least to strive for some more substantive reconstruction of American society which salvages the best of N. T. Gration's hopes while avoiding both his naiveté and his failures. Black America's one longing has been for equality—and it was for integration as long as that seemed the best means to achieve it. If whites had not confused integration with race-mixing, or equality with an alleged black desire to dish out to whites what whites had handed out to blacks for three hundred years (although it's easy to see how a guilt-ridden white conscience might assume such), the whole story might have been different.

N. T. Gration is dead, but before either white bigots or black militants begin to dance on his grave, we might all do well to ponder the plight in which his passing has left us. For all the abundant promises and lack of progress which marked N. T. Gration's era, there was a certain quality of saneness that presided during the discussions and negotiations of that period —or if saneness is too innocuous a phrase, at least one could hear what the other side was saying, even though one would have preferred the opposition to be saying something more substantive. Today, however, both sides in the controversy are shouting semi-hysterically—and one suspects it is for their own rather than the other's edification. Accordingly, the intrepid leader of this nation, having gained for himself a four year, rent-free lease on the nation's most prestigious piece of residential property, has proposed with some wisdom and appropriateness that we all lower our voices a decimal or two so that we begin once more to listen to what each other has to say.

The black populace in America, which has been a strong advocate of rent subsidies but was singularly unenthusiastic about giving the nation's Chief Executive any such boon, has been listening to hear what he might say about America's Number One domestic problem. They've watched him fly all over the globe, offering peace, hope and prosperity to the rest of the world. They've read press comments of his helicopter rides over the nation's capital to observe its traffic problems. They've witnessed his unrelenting efforts to curb inflation by passionately pursuing the classic economic dogma that when there is too much money floating around, it means too many people (especially black people) are working. They've observed his diligent and almost daily attention to questions of national security, military preparedness and moon flights but they have yet to hear one, single, solitary word from the White House—even from a press secretary—about the one-tenth of the nation who want in on American society.

And so we've run the gamut in America: from rational discourse and no movement, to strident shouting and no movement, to the current, presidentially requested silence—and no movement! It doesn't leave much in the way of intelligent options, and there is good reason to suspect that this is precisely where we're heading in America—toward an era that will rival the days of the cavemen for ignorance, superstition and savagery. But since that's where this whole business got started, perhaps the second time around we can hope for some slight improvements. Who knows? Perhaps cavemen had a cure for racism that has escaped the subtle sophistication of our more modern minds!

# V

# Why Integration Failed . . .
# Or What We Discovered
# about Mediocrity

One of the most important discoveries that black people have made as a result of the racial struggle in America is how many important and lucrative jobs are held in the white world by frightfully mediocre white people. It is a discovery born of the integration era and the decades of pressure by blacks to get into the mainstream of American society, spurred on by white insistence that "qualified" black men and women would have no difficulty being accepted as equals in the employment market. "Qualified" in this instance, however, has turned out to mean being twice as good as any white person holding the same job, and for the first fifty years of this century has resulted in black people going to college in order to get jobs as elevator operators and postal clerks.

Because black people didn't know any better, they assumed that the plums of employment hanging lavishly from the trees of business and industry could be plucked only by the most brilliant and talented of whites, whose European background, Mayflower descendency and Dartmouth degrees made them natural heirs to such ripe opportunities. Blacks, therefore, were inclined to overflow with gratitude for the chance simply to work in the company mills and foundries, for hot and unhealthy though they were, they did offer the distinct advantage of relatively steady work (i.e., it beat chopping cotton for three months out of the year) and relatively good wages (i.e., twice as much as the pay for cotton-chopping). Blacks never dreamed that they might be able to perform effectively as first-line supervisors, or as assistant managers of all sorts and descriptions, or in marketing, administration, sales, public relations and the like, especially when personnel managers were trying to convince black job seekers that good education and good breeding *were* essential to acquiring such jobs. (Translated into black requirements, good education meant having a Harvard PhD for any job above foreman, while good breeding meant not having membership in any civil rights organization more militant than the Urban League.) Imagine, therefore, the sheer shock and amazement that gripped black people when the barriers to equal opportunity were finally lowered a decade or so ago, and blacks got their first real look at these white symbols of good education and good breeding who had been holding down all the plush, well-paying white collar jobs in business and industry.

That's where the white Establishment made its first big mistake! It let black people in on its nine-to-five, martini-before-lunch, flirt-with-the-secretaries world, giving in the process a first-hand glimpse at this enchanting, affluent, hypertensive, fight-your-way-to-the-top, white life-style which blacks had tried to enter(grate) for so long. We finally got that magnificent opportunity for which we had so unceasingly struggled: to work side by side with guys who spend eight hours a day looking busy, three and a half hours commuting back and forth from suburbia, another two (if there's daylight) hours fighting crabgrass and the rest of the time lying awake wondering when "they" will move in the subdivision.

Nevertheless, we treasured the anticipated opportunity of those enlightening eight hours, the chance to learn the secret of white success. After the first eight months, we wondered when the coffee break conversation would shift from booze, broads and baseball (we already knew about these basics of life but we assumed our white co-workers were just trying to make us feel at home). We sat patiently, waiting to hear penetrating assessments of the population explosion, the war in

Vietnam or the plight of the cities, anxious to learn the meaning of the Dow-Jones Industrial Average or the significance of the Gross National Product. But eighteen months later, we were discovering that booze, broads and baseball are all "they" have to talk about, and that not very expertly.

Inevitably the conversation finally shifted to that all-consuming white topic of "the color problem," usually initiated by some subtle, cryptic observation on how convenient it must be to be black and not have to comb your hair in the morning or what a shame it is some way can't be found to stop ADC mothers from having babies. Black workers quickly discover in such situations that there is no effective way to turn such discussion to more timely topics, and that the sooner one gets it over with, the better. So with a pained attempt to appear grateful that such profound interest was being displayed in our welfare—a consistently recurring theme in all conversations with whites and not to be confused with the state of our well-being —we began that ancient process of educating white folk about the facts of black life. We created elaborate explanations for the mystique of our congenitally-inherited rhythm which reveals itself in our universally known abilities to sing and dance, we denied heatedly that all blacks are Baptists or Methodists, and we smiled sensually at those suggestive inquiries that sought to discover the secret of our sexual prowess. Having thus exhausted the principal areas of white interest in black affairs, we then faced the option of returning to the B syndrome (booze, broads and baseball) or of avoiding such inane matters and thereby gaining a reputation of being "uppity."

No one has fully realized the impossible position into which that black generation was placed, the generation on whose shoulders fell the task of integrating the white world. Subject to demands from whites that they be superblacks on the one hand, and the suspicion from fellow blacks that their success in the white world was somehow at the cost of their blackness on the other, these racial misfits have turned out to be the prime casualties of America's racial dilemma. They exchanged chitterlings for cheese fondue, Baptist fervor for

Episcopalian respectability, and Little Stevie Wonder for Caesar Franck. Occasionally on weekends in their integrated neighborhoods they reverted to the old folkways, but they were careful to cook their barbecue in covered outdoor pits (and never on Saturdays if the neighborhood was still Jewish) or, even more thoughtfully, to buy it from some well-known joint in the ghetto. They joined block clubs (where they were immediately elected club secretary to see if they could read and write—but, for some strange reason, never treasurer), learned to play bridge and discovered the art of shopping in suburban supermarkets where the food is fresher, the prices cheaper and the service immeasurably better, provided they could live with the disadvantage of not finding a wide assortment of pig's feet and black-eyed peas.

But times change, and with them yesterday's heroes become today's martyrs and tomorrow's tragedies. In this case, however, the tragedy lies not so much in what the integrating black gave up (pig's feet aren't really that appetizing) as it does in the strange level of ordinariness (mediocrity) they entered in the white world. Having been continually told by whites and by anxious blacks as well that he must be twice as smart as the average white person in order to succeed, the black integrationist logically assumed this meant that he was only half as bright as the nearest white. So he pushed himself through school, studied twice as hard, got all the honors he could collect and then went job-hunting only to find, if he was successful, that all the time he had been preparing for competition with guys who were no smarter than he was! And to add insult to injury, he now found himself overtrained for the entry level job he had been obligingly given, smarter than his supervisor (who also recognized this fact and immediately became the source of rumors that the blacks are trying to take over), and infinitely beyond the tastes, perceptions, insights and intelligence of his co-workers whose big blow for equality would come six months later when they would graciously invite our racial pacesetter to have coffee at the same table with them.

## I

Mediocrity has been a major factor in the system that runs the white world for generations, but whites have been too arrogant to admit it and blacks have been too ignorant of white ways to understand it—until now. Blacks have been blinded by the brilliance and savoir faire of the Kennedys and Rockefellers in government, forgetting that they don't run the United States any more than some six-figure automotive tycoon runs the car industry he heads. Government, car corporations, banks, schools, hospitals and even universities are managed by mediocre minds and administered on the famous formula that work expands to fit the time allotted in which to do it. The white world has even perfected a system by which it consecrates mediocrity—in government it's called civil service, one of the most imaginative devices ever conceived by the mind of man to thwart innovation and efficiency. The historians tell us that civil service was a response to the evils of the spoils system, inaugurated at the turn of the present century to protect the populace from politicians who persisted in filling public offices with their incompetent friends and relatives. What the proponents of the civil service system failed to recognize, however, is that by the time they set out to reform the abuses of political patronage, a second law of human dynamics had come into effect—work contracts to fit the capacity of the persons doing it. The singular effect of civil service, therefore, has been to freeze job functions at the level of incompetence represented by the persons in government when civil service was first introduced, thereby giving America that great system of democracy known as government of the people, for the people, and by incompetents.

As a consequence, the most serious and far-reaching decisions in American society today are being made and managed by the most incredible collection of short-sighted bureaucratic minds in the history of world civilization. The most tyrannical period of medieval history would not rival today's administrative bumbling, if for no other reason than that of sheer numbers. At the very most, the medievalists had only one whimsical character to deal with, and they could always hope (or pray) that war or the plague might bring a more enlightened heir to the throne. But not so in modern America, where presidents, senators, congressmen, judges, mayors and councilmen come and go—while society staggers and stumbles onward, occasionally prodded but more frequently misdirected by that countless throng of nameless public servants, protected throughout retirement if not all eternity by that sacrosanct system which is civil service.

Black people have sought to penetrate this maze of governmental administration in the mistaken belief that they are entitled to the same security it has afforded white people all these years. Their efforts became intensified when they began to discover how civil service has really operated as a sort of official protection racket for white nepotism—examine, for example, any big city police or fire department, budget bureau or parks' commission and you will find the payroll roster reads like somebody's family tree, with brothers, sons and nephews all over the place. (The same charge could be leveled against two-thirds of the building trades unions, but the author avoids doing so since some of his best friends are unionists.) And the system works as well as it does because those already in the system manipulate it, all of which makes for a neat little employment monopoly more selective than membership in the Daughters of the American Revolution.

Fearless blacks tackled this, however, as they have so many of America's inconsistencies in the past, only to hear anguished cries from within the system that "blacks are trying to lower standards"—to lower standards, mind you, when all that blacks hoped to do (besides getting a decent-paying job commensurate with all that education whitey keeps telling them to get) was to infuse a little fresh blood into the operation. For as everyone knows, constant in-breeding produces an inferior strain of anything—except, curiously, racism which seems to grow stronger the more it is ingrained from generation to generation.

II

There is little wonder, therefore, that today's racial dilemma has produced such a vibrant and virulent crop of black militants and that they are drawn (much as they would like to forget or ignore the fact) overwhelmingly from the ranks of yesterday's ardent integrationists. Caught between white promises and black hopelessness, choosing to trust in the white promises as against black futility, these are the generation who have been so consistently disappointed in white America. They've played its game, according to its rules, but they haven't been allowed to win the prize. But what is perhaps far more revealing, they've competed just long and hard enough to have concluded that the prize isn't really worth it after all.

And so the militants turn inward toward what may be a far more meaningful, pleasurable, less-hung-up life-style within their own communities. Some are so convinced of the imminent collapse of white culture that they opt for their own nation; to speak of integration to them is to invite them to climb on board a sinking ship. Others prefer to let white racism take its natural course, which means that it is only a matter of time until all whites have left the cities (except for a few, die-hard liberals who never have presented much for blacks or whites to worry about) and then blacks can come into their own.

White liberals, caught between their own guilt-ridden failures and the rising black spirit of self-determination, have up until now languished in uncertainty about which way to jump next. They can still make a pitch for integration, however, feeble though it might be, if they are bold enough to point out to the black militants that the cities they hope to take over or the South in which the new black nation is to be formed have already had it. Black power will prove as ineffective in saving cities from water and air pollution, labor strikes, dwindling fiscal resouces, decaying schools, rising crime and spreading slums as white power has been effective in creating these problems. As for the South, every black person in his right mind is trying desperately to get out of there; leading them back again will call for a bigger trick than Moses accomplished in parting the Red Sea.

The only hope, therefore, lies in white liberals and blacks striking a bargain, one that will have to be infinitely more ingenious than that which will be proposed later for blacks and white conservatives. For openers, white liberals will probably have to accede to a black demand that they make a public stand for intermarriage. (It should be noted in advance that blacks won't make this demand seriously; it will simply be a way of testing white liberal sincerity. On the other hand, if white liberals take it seriously, as they seem inclined to take any black demand these days, it will knock the wind right out of the "black is beautiful" movement and give blacks and whites alike a new and common theme song—"gray is great.") Then, in recognition of the fact that blacks have been overpreparing themselves all these years for integrating with white mediocrity, whites will have to content themselves with black misgivings about "lowering standards" whenever whites apply for jobs in what will naturally be black-run operations.

Finally there is the matter of reparations. It is significant that the famous Foreman demands (notoriously underpriced, by the way) were directed at the white churches, and not because (as several white theologians, overawed with this welcomed recognition of their institutional existence, mistakenly assumed) the churches are wealthy, powerful or significant, but rather because the most hysterical segment of white liberalism can be found within the ranks of the church. It is significant that reparation demands were not tacked to the door of the Chase Manhattan Bank or the gates of Fort Knox or even the local office of the Internal Revenue Service, any one of which would have taken appropriate steps to ship the reparations demanders off to Vietnam, and to the thickest part of the fighting at that. To the contrary, it was with brilliant and calculated forethought that the churches were singled out as the one institution in American society upon which to make such wide-sweeping financial demands. For only from the church could one anticipate sophisticated and profound theological position papers in response to such a move, seeking to probe the Judaeo-Christian dimensions, the socio-ethical implications and the doctrinal imperatives implicit in such "a recognition of the churches and synagogues as the decisive centers of culture" in America. If the Foreman Manifesto had demanded that churches and synagogues castrate their clergy as reparation for the rape of black women during the slave era, some theologian, bishop or enlightened liberal layman would have striven to discover a theological rationale for accepting the legitimacy of the demand.

Instead, there are more sensible options. White churches could pay the head price demanded and force the black strategists back into a huddle to think up a better one. This at least would buy time, with the added advantage of arriving at a settlement before the price goes up. Or the churches could ignore the Manifesto, find their houses of worship picketed by fierce looking blacks, and then go underground, which, reminiscent of the early days of the church, might greatly improve the quality of their spiritual life and commitments. But by far the most effective response would be to agree to the proposed head price in return for a black moratorium on writing theologies of violence, which would permit white churchmen to turn their attention to more serious theological questions, and black churchmen to get back to concerns about their flocks, who are not about to settle three hundred years of American racism for the cheap price of fifteen dollars apiece.

# VI

# So What Do We Do Next?
# (Guidelines for Black Radicals)

It is absolutely amazing the amount of sheer terror a handful of black students can create these days. All that is needed is the gab and the garb—or, as we say in the ghetto, "put on the robe and rap, baby, and you can scare 'the Man' out of his white, middle-class wits." Not, of course, that we've just learned the secret of terrorizing white people; actually this has been a sort of black specialty for decades.

Black people probably first discovered this useful little device a few years after Nat Turner's famous escapade, in which a handful of black slaves decided they had had enough of the barbarism of the white system of slavery and proceeded to dispatch a few symbols of the slave establishment to that "Sweet By And By" about which the whites were always singing and praying so enthusiastically. It was unquestionably a sad event, but hardly of the quality or quantity of those episodes in which the villain was Wyatt Earp or the Clancy brothers or Bugsy Moran or Al Capone or a hundred other colorful (and white) characters in American history.

And yet, in the aftermath of the Turner rebellion, the whole South hit the panic button. They passed laws forbidding more than five blacks to assemble at one time (recent, post-riot legislation of the same order was actually based, therefore, on excellent legal precedent); they made it illegal to teach slaves to read and write (especially the Bible, since it was presumed that Turner, a black preacher, got all those crazy notions about human dignity from the Good Book) and forbade slave assemblies for worship unless a white person was present (guarding thereby against any discussion of such liberal doctrines as liberty, equality and fraternity).

The Nat Turner episode and its aftermath left a residue of black fear in white minds which whites, over one hundred years later, have never managed to overcome. And partly because of this fear, white America has isolated and insulated itself as carefully and systematically as possible from physical contact with black people; it is probably why the ultimate in white fear is the most intimate possible contact with blacks—intermarriage (which, on the surface at least, is just a bit irrational; after all, who ever carries a razor to bed with him?).

One can see this fear, which at points can create a kind of catatonic state in its white victims, if a black person steps on an elevator occupied by a white person. If they both ride more than five floors together, the white person can appear, in that brief time, to experience a panic-stricken paralysis. If a black person stands next to one on a subway platform, or sits next to one on a bus or across the table in a crowded restaurant, all the symptoms of shock will appear: beads of perspiration, heavy sighing, loss of appetite.

White liberals have assumed that many of the difficulties arise because of lack of contact between the races. Surely, they postulate, as we get to know each other more and better (as if there were an automatic cause-effect relationship in such a process) and as we find out we have the same interests (e.g., finding out why all blacks are such good dancers and drive Cadillacs) and that we all really have the same goals in life (getting black people to "do something" about the crime problem and welfare chiselers), we can diminish the fear and increase good will among all men (if, of course, we're willing to give this whole thing time).

The history of the half-century in which black people played this brotherhood game according to white liberal rules has been recounted earlier. Blacks tried to make themselves, in appearance, demeanor and desire, as little frightening to white people as possible. Blacks dressed like white peo-

ple, combed their hair like white people, and learned to talk
and eat like white people. Blacks even learned (may the good
Lord forgive us) to laugh at white psychopathic, sex-ridden
jokes (in which blacks usually played the leading roles). And
what did it get us? A multi-million dollar hair-straighten-
ing industry (the biggest black-owned business in America,
next to life insurance and funeral parlors) and ulcers, but not
a solitary, significant improvement in the plight of the black
masses in this nation.

No wonder then that blacks have decided to reverse roles
for a while. If we cannot communicate with white society by
being as unobtrusively Negro as we can, then let's try to raise
the issue by being as abrasively black as possible. The present
danger, however, is that blacks will depend upon mere happen-
stance to get mileage out of this move. We've had enough recent
experience in abrasiveness to perfect this latest ploy into a
sophisticated strategy. (Note: White readers may skip, if they
wish to, the latter part of this chapter, while the author dis-
courses for the next few pages for the benefit of his black
brothers.)

I

Taking a page from the experiences of our young, black revolutionaries who have been actively "liberating" the centers
of power in American society (student unions, the private
washrooms of university presidents and abandoned church build-
ings), we should recognize that Anglomania can best be tempted,
triggered and tormented if blacks pursue the following simple guidelines:

* Develop the art of looking mean as an initial and essential part of the strategy; whitey is so accustomed to the Ste-
pin Fetchet, fawning, subservient grin that he becomes totally immobilized at the sight of a hostile-looking black
face. Under no circumstances should you lapse into a laugh,
even upon hearing the news that whitey will fund your Af-

ro-American Society for the Promotion of White Guilt and buy the first one thousand copies of your mimeographed autobiography (which retails for $6.95 a copy).

* As part of the terrorist outfit, be sure at all times to wear dark sun glasses, known to all true brothers as "shades." This not only adds to the overall sinisterness of your appearance, but it also prevents "the Man" from seeing your eyes (which may be bloodshot from lack of sleep due to the previous night's planning strategy meeting, or from last night's gig— both of which may have been the same occasion) and consequently leaves him to wallow in his uncertainty about how really mad you might be.

* Whenever engaged in conversation with whitey, keep your hands in constant motion. The diversion will diminish the possibility that he will catch onto the patness of your argument, but, of far greater importance, whitey will expect a razor to flash forth from those moving hands at any moment. You can be certain that he will not move a muscle until you have finished your argument.

* It is also essential to know how to distort history, a relatively easy accomplishment since whitey knows next to nothing about the American historical experience and even less about any black involvement therein. Begin, therefore, by bedazzling "the Man" with a few obscure black names, dates and circumstances (be sure to avoid Cab Calloway and Joe Louis since these famed symbols of black pride and progress are well known in white America). You can anticipate a look of ignorant amazement as you recount famous blacks who excelled in something besides dancing and sports. With this obvious advantage, you can proceed to bombard your listener with sweeping accusations concerning the role of his honky religion, facist military complex and bourgeois economic system in the exploitation of black people whose cause is synonymous with those of Africans, Arabs, Peruvians and mainland Chinese peoples, whether the latter realize it or not.

Pause to appropriately point out how whitey has been beguiled all these years by the Thomistic (not to be confused with Aquinas; this scholarly reference points to more recent intellectuals whose common lot is that they are Negroid and make more than $10,000 a year) sophistry of traitors to the black cause who advocated such treasonous notions as a biracial society. Finally, with a few appropriate quotes from Mao Tse Tung and Che Guevera, whose compassion for and insight into the problem and hopes of black America are so widely renowned, you can end with a flourish on some ringing Third World revolutionary theme, all of which is guaranteed to raise ultimate terror (along with gun sales and Republican votes) in white America. The basic point to keep in mind, of course, is that the truth about white America is never sufficient; it has to be distorted to be believed or to have effect.

* Finally, remember that white guilt can be parlayed into the best of all possible worlds. Your most susceptible victim, therefore, is not the die-hard bigot who is equally adept at looking mean, prone to violence and capable of distorting facts. Instead, concentrate your energies on that soft-hearted (and soft-headed), very confused, well-intentioned, guilty-as-sin white liberal. He eagerly awaits your onslaught, will wallow in every angry accusation, and, if you can hold up under his verbal acts of contrition, may give you in the bargain a few self-inflicted barbs that escaped even your angry imagination.

## II

The reasons that white liberals are so vulnerable to the guilt-producing assaults of angry blacks are not grounded solely in the bare fact that whites have an abundance of history about which to properly feel guilt; they also lie in the deep recesses of that peculiar religious heritage which produced white, liberal America. While most white liberals would either deny it

or prefer not to be reminded of the fact, they are nevertheless
social heirs of that most magnificent of theological traditions,
American Calvinism. And for a system designed to produce
guilt of all kinds, there is no equal. Witness, for example, the
unexcelled achievements of the Puritans in this regard. American Puritanism, as the peculiar product of European Calvinism
and the American wilderness, was not the dour, straight-laced
life-style that most moderns have in mind when they use the
term "Puritan"—frequently (and ignorantly) in derision. They
may have been a sober lot on Sunday (as their spiritual heirs
have tried in vain to keep the rest of us ever since), but during
the week they took their Protestant ethic seriously: they worked
energetically, drank freely and played enthusiastically. They
did have one major hang-up, however, as Hawthorne has never
let the world forget, and that was sex. This popular pastime,
when combined with a humorless view of human existence that
Calvinism is wont to encourage, can produce an abundant
amount of guilt in the best of societies. In American culture
it reached its zenith and might have totally overwhelmed the
modern white mind, had not Freud and his followers created
the persuasively powerful antidote of psychiatry and psycho-
analysis, and had black people not provided appropriate models
of sublimation.

The point is that whites in general and white liberals in
particular have the trinitarian forces of their American history,
their sexual proclivities and their theological presuppositions
all going for them when it comes to producing a guilty conscience. Black strategy therefore should not be wasted on producing more of the same. All that is needed is to enlarge and
enhance it, and forces far more powerful than black anger or
white compassion will do the rest. For properly-kindled white
guilt becomes a veritable forest fire of self-recrimination, self-
renunication and passionate commitment to worthless causes
—all in the name of righting the wrongs of the past. Once
moved to this state of remorse, the white liberal will do anything to gain the regard of his black brothers. He will submit
to any demand no matter how wild, accept any verbal abuse
no matter how crude, and condone any conduct no matter how

barbaric. For so struck is he by the sins of his fathers that he is determined not to prolong the offense, even if it means sacrificing his good sense in the bargain. His fathers have eaten sour grapes, and his teeth have been so set on edge that they will chatter uncontrollably at the sight or sound of an angry black demand.

Not that the white liberal is prepared to do anything significant, mind you; this is the mistaken notion harbored by a small, vociferous and extremely misguided group of black activists who mistake verbal repentance for a change of heart. One would think that after a decade of white liberal attempts to pass open-housing ordinances, black activists would know better by now. But since the real mentality of the white liberal seems to be lost on them, let the true nature of white liberal racial feelings now be made clear. For American Calvinism has not only contributed to the enormous guilt feelings of white America, it has also produced a strange reaction—a phenomenon which is best described as racial masochism. In some unexplainable manner, whites who suffer from this malady feel expiated on racial issues simply if they are verbally pilloried and castigated by blacks, and the more militant the better, as though if one subjects oneself to the personal pain and anguish of listening to a black harangue, one somehow thereby cleanses oneself of responsibility for doing anything about the black problem. It is almost as though the racial masochist is saying: "No one in white America is listening to my angry black brother; all my white cohorts turn him off, and I, only I, have the guts (somehow initially indistinguishable from fear but quickly becoming escalated into courage and strength) to listen to him. And since that is more than anyone else is doing, it will suffice for the present."

### III

If our current strategy of abrasive blackness is to get results, therefore, we must not count too heavily on it to produce any meaningful results in white, liberal circles. In fact, our best hope might be to strike an alliance with white, conservative America whom we can at least confront on substantive issues. Enthralled as the conservative is with the good old days when life was simple, cities were small and we blacks knew our place, we can probably strike several very effective and practical bargains. We could, for example, declare our non-interest in that throwback to nineteenth-century America—the suburb— in exchange for preemptive rights to the nation's cities, and then charge tolls on all the freeway routes into the centers of the metropolis which are being built to give suburbanites the luxury of enjoying the city's pleasures while simultaneously escaping its responsibilities. This new source of revenue might solve the fiscal problems of the major urban areas or else keep "the Man" in his semi-rural place, where he belongs. We would also probably find that the white conservative is willing to be- lieve us when we announce, for the umpteenth time, that we are no longer interested in integrated schools—something that for the life of us we cannot get across to white liberals. We could even promise to discourage our sons from marrying their daughters, if they can assure us that their daughters will not marry our sons, a pact that is certain to bring joy and relief to the white, conservative mind.

If all else fails, we have a sure-fire strategy with white con- servatives that is virtually guaranteed to get immediate capit- ulation on any point which we wish to demand or negotiate. The lives and fortunes of conservative, middle-class, white America still turn on their black, domestic (you should pardon the expression because most of them are over 40) "girls" who clean their homes, do their shopping, cook their meals, disci- pline their children and listen, with an endurance beyond de- scription, to their endless misgivings about "what Negroes want." All we have to do is call a nationwide strike of black domestics and we can bring white America to its knees—or else watch it slowly starve to death!

# VII

# Sex and the White Racist . . .
# Single, Married or Otherwise

One day some enterprising researcher will really expose the ultimate in hang-ups for whites and hopefully tell the world why it is that white people are so obsessed with one of life's great pleasures, which for them is such a uniquely white problem. For in typically Caucasoid fashion, whites write books, watch movies, tell jokes, create institutes and lead crusades to reform school curricula, all centered on the one overriding theme of sex. And because it is such a problem for whitey, he can neither understand nor appreciate the fact that it is not a "problem" for blacks. (In spite of the increasing imitation of the white world, we blacks have yet to produce a black version of the Kinsey Report, which Moynihan keeps thinking we need, nor are there any prominent black members of the burgeoning Sex Education in the School committees).

It is reasonable to conclude (if you think white, of course) that blacks are either culturally immoral, congenitally superior or intellectually incapable of realizing what a profound emotional and interpersonal problem sex is! That we're ignorant on the subject no one has had the brashness to suggest; white infatuation with statistics being what it is, it would be hard to handle our birth rate on this assumption. Cultural immorality has long been a favorite white rationale recently raised to the level of scientific objectivity by the astounding, government-sponsored, research finding that fathers in our black families are conspicuously absent (although how that biologically permits immorality is a mystery).

61

The third option (that we are congenitally superior) lingers as a strong suspicion, however, and it manages to surface most frequently at integrated cocktail parties when whites get tanked or familiar enough (one suspects a cause-effect relationship) to tell their latest funny story. Invariably, the theme is sex, the characters are black and the point of the joke (when there is one) is our cavalier attitude toward or proficiency in matters sexual.

No black person will ever confirm whether there is truth behind the legend, for as long as whites *think* there is, they have something to worry over and we have something worth laughing about. That we could so easily and innocently contribute to white anxiety and so effectively nourish white guilt gives us a source of racial pride, whether the reasons have a basis in fact or not.

# I

Dealing honestly with such a delicate theme as sex, which is simultaneously repressed and exploited to such an enormous degree in white America, calls for unusual care and caution. But on the theory that black Americans perhaps can make a significant contribution to the discussion of this problem, it might be instructive to examine the black perspective on this critical white dilemma. For if whites had not become so sensitive to the sophistry of the psychiatric guild, whose work in large measure has provided a scientific rationale for the sex obsession (and an enormous clientele in the bargain), they might have been able to view sex from the simple vantage point that blacks do: the happy consequence of a biological habit and good interpersonal relations! Sex for black people is as natural as eating, sleeping and sweating, and since whitey has kept us in inferior schools and been teaching us manual trades all these years, we have been saved (thank God) from learning all that classical Greek jazz about oedipal complexes, libidinal desires and the like (although certain forms of extraordinarily crude ghetto language might indicate we had grasped the meaning if not the message of these complex concepts—a classic proof of the first axiom in race relations which asserts that blacks are learning all the worst habits of white folks). It frightens us to think how hung-up *we* might be if we knew how many of our problems—real, imaginary or otherwise—stemmed from faulty toilet training!

Our black psychiatrists, on the other hand, have performed a much more valuable service for us. Having mastered the professional (and enormously esoteric) jargon of the psychiatric guild, they have turned the simplicities of sex into a process by which we assert our manhood and thereby have skillfully managed to convince us that what we mistook for a universal birthright is in fact some kind of acquired racial uniqueness that is all our own. Black pride will not be thwarted, and since sex is the only area in which white folks have been willing to give us credit for some know-how, who can blame us if we try to make the most of it?

In earlier and less complex times, however, and among those sections of the black populace as yet untainted by the continual temptation to make eternal verities out of obvious facts, sex remains precisely that—an obvious and delightful fact, unencumbered and uncomplicated by all the psychiatric, mid-Victorian, puritanical, theologically straitlaced nonsense with which the modern white world has surrounded and updated it. Blacks, as everyone knows, are great Bible readers with an especial affinity for the Old Testament and its drama, intrigue, suffering, sorrow . . . and sex. Black religion dwells persistently (and at times amusingly) on these themes in which the struggle of black people in America becomes an historical rerun of the saga of the children of Israel. There are indeed prominent black theologians on the scene today who argue with considerable cleverness that the history of Israel in biblical times is the history of black people—an assertion which, if true, gives the twin weight of antiquity and divine sanction to the black outlook and experience. At the very least, it suggests that a healthy outlook on matters sexual has some important historical precedents. For it takes a pretty wild imagination to beat the nocturnal habits of the Davids and Solomons of old who apparently managed relatively well without the insights of Freud or the pacesetting pressures of *Playboy* magazine.

Their spiritual successors, however, have not fared as well. Somewhere between Solomon and Sigmund Freud, sex became synonymous with sin and its practice an unfortunate but necessary process in procreation rather than a pleasurable pursuit. The blame for this tragic turn of events has often been laid at the theological feet of St. Paul who has been accused by his detractors of being everything from a divorced cynic to a congenital woman-hater. But to identify any one villain in the history of white hang-ups about sex is to let the whole of white culture off too easily. For what is most impressive about white folks and sex is how reflective the latter has traditionally been of white attitudes toward life and other people in general—cold, detached, unfeeling and terribly suspicious. It is almost as though white people would rather be white than be people, a devastating indictment to make of an entire populace but one nevertheless painfully evident, at least when white living is viewed from a black perspective.

Currently, popular white culture, as reflected in magazines and the movies, conversation and night club routines, has developed an additional extremist stance on sex, so that now whites either pretend that sex doesn't exist or portray life as though sex is all there is to it. Only the advertising world with its copious use of luscious models to make sales pitches for everything from antacid relievers to plumbing appliances has learned to treat the subject of sex with subtlety, probably because it has recognized that sex as an obsession in the white world plays second fiddle only to one other popular pastime—making money.

Extremism for white Americans is not really new or surprising—on sex or any other subject; indeed, the extremes between which white attitudes on sex swing are comparable only to their extremes on matters of race (which is why, dear reader, the issues of sex and racism are so intimately—you should pardon the expression—and inextricably intertwined). No white person is ever neutral on either subject, and those most hung-up on the former are likely to be most solid on the latter. In fact (and this would probably please old Sigmund immensely) it is interesting to note that the conservative white mentality which vigorously opposes sex education in the schools turns out in many instances to be that which, with equal vigor, proposes shipping all blacks back to Africa. If ever we resolve the difficulties of whites on sex, perhaps we can simultaneously unravel the riddle of racism as well.

Compare, if you will, the nonchalant, easy-going, cavalier attitude on sex that pervades black society. For sex among blacks is symbolic of a life-style, one which has seen such a consistent denial of most of life's material pursuits that it has forced us back upon the one hope and happiness that we could count on—a deeply personal relationship with one another. It has produced a warmth and congeniality in the black spirit (which whites have mistaken for rhythm and sensualness); it permits us to enjoy physical contact (did you ever notice how black men kiss women unreservedly in public?). All this is a manifestation of the deep affection and appreciation life has taught us to have for genuine human relationships. The simple difference is that for blacks sex is a natural and exquisite expression of living, while for whites living appears to be an obsessive and panic-striken exhibition of sex—and thereby hangs the tale.

## II

Relating the vagaries of sex to the problems of white racism may seem to call for a considerable stretch of the imagination; however, if the truth be known, they are almost inseparable. Probe the fears of most whites regarding blacks and you will find the heart of the matter resides in and revolves around the imagined horror of sexual contact. This fear reveals itself in various and curious ways, not all of which involve the ultimate in terror for white parents (i.e., fear that their daughter might marry one). Recently, for example, a small university town in a midwestern American state lived through the horror of a savage series of sex slayings involving some seven, attractive, young, white, university coeds over a period of two years. The seventh slaying resulted in an arrest of a black suspect whom the press immediately portrayed as a brutal, callous, and savage sex maniac with a history of sexual perversion (the suspect had served a prison sentence for rape). Shortly after his arrest, an eighth sex murder occurred and a white suspect was arrested—a university senior who, at least according to the press reports, seemed much more intimately connected with the whole series of slayings than the black suspect. The compassion with which the white arrestee was treated by the press, however, bordered on the nauseous. He was a "quiet, studious, fraternity man" with an exemplary academic record whose neighbors thought the world of him and whom no one ever suspected might be involved in such a horrible affair.

Or take the modern film world with its renown for honest, candid and uninhibited treatment of real life. Hollywood has dealt (magnificently at times) with every controversial subject known to man, from lesbianism to insanity among the military, but it has yet to treat authentically the issue which everyone whispers about and sees on the streets, at the theaters or in restaurants, but one whose existence very few whites wish to admit—interracial love. (Interracial sex, it should be noted, Hollywood deals with endlessly; one can hardly pass a fifth-rate movie house marquee that is not advertising "White Mother—Black Baby" or some equally inspiring theme.) But the recognition of the possibility that a white person could love a black person is so alien to the American film world that it has yet to be sensitively and honestly treated in a good movie.

Those who dissent from this accusation will immediately drag "Guess Who's Coming to Dinner?" into the discussion as Exhibit Number One for the defense. However, black people found this film to be much more pertinent in what it said about white attitudes toward race than anything it might have tried to say about interracial love. The black character in the plot, you will recall, was carefully portrayed as a superblack; he was a brilliant young M.D. and the world's leading (in fact, *only*) authority on some rare tropical disease. He was a cat (as we blacks would admiringly say) who would have been a welcomed addition to anyone's household—as rare as the tropical disease on which he was so expert. The plot of the picture, as black folks saw it, was exactly that—a non-too-clever plot to convince blacks, once again, that if we are the best of the very best, nothing (not even white women) are beyond our dreams. Accordingly, white audiences who viewed this flick could go home secure in the notion that if some black ever came calling on their daughter, he would have three PhD's in subjects they couldn't even pronounce, and blacks went back to the ghetto assured once again that the ordinary, average, hard working black doesn't stand a chance at anything—not even in a world of ordinary, average white people.

Like every other dilemma of modern times, the problem of sex and racism is rooted in history. It was America's fate and fortune (fortunate for whites, fatal for blacks) to be colonized by immigrants from the British Isles and from northern Europe in the seventeenth and eighteenth centuries. Unlike the Spanish and Portuguese who settled South America, the American colonizers had no prior experience with dark-skinned peoples; they therefore developed a colorphobia that has haunted the white American mentality ever since. In contrast, the Spanish and Portuguese, with their geographic proximity to the African continent and their centuries of experience with dark skins, were able to avoid, for the most part, the simple equation of blackness with dullness, ignorance, inferiority and immorality. In addition, Roman Catholicism, with its widespread contacts with peoples and nations all over the then-known world, in its better moments served as a check of sorts on the attitudes of its Spanish-Portuguese colonizers toward slavery in South America (i.e., it didn't check the development of slavery, but it did help, by its insistence that slavery was a condition that could befall any man, to thwart the North American notion that slavery was synonymous with blackness. This may have been poor theology but it made for exceptionally good race relations).

The result of all this is simply that white racism, in countries

like Brazil, is virtually unknown. Brazil has its class conflicts
and an extraordinary amount of poverty, but poverty in Brazil
is not a by-product of race, whatever else its origins might be.
All of this leads one to conclude (with apologies to all my Protestant cohorts) that if this country had been settled by
Spanish and Portuguese Catholics instead of English Calvin-
ists and German Lutherans, we blacks might not be in the mess
we are today!

If white racism has its roots in American Protestantism, it
merely provides American Protestants with an additional
rationale for eradicating it. And if they wish to take up this
difficult task, they should have no hesitancy in calling upon
their Catholic confreres for help, since contemporary Catholicism is not exactly a racial utopia either—proof positive of the
second law of religious relations, i.e., Catholics are learning all
the worst habits of Protestants, an axiom of ecumenism which
conservative Catholics have long suspected but one which they
have erroneously applied to the wrong situation. Perhaps somewhere between Protestant Puritanism and Catholic creeds on
contraception, blacks can provide the basis for a new theology
of sex which (God willing and Paul VI permitting) will contribute simultaneously to the advance of ecumenism and the
decline of racism in American society.

Until that blessed day arrives (if ever it does) we will have
to contend with the reality of the enormous, deep-seated, obsessive white fear of blacks, a fear rooted in sexual fantasy and
revealed in a thousand and one situations in American life.
Arnold Toynbee's classic solution of mass intermarriage might
resolve the problem, only none of us alive today (or our great
grandchildren for that matter) would be around to see the results. Shipping all blacks back to Africa wouldn't quite do it
either; thanks to the "messing around" of Southern white men
over the centuries, so many blacks have gotten white enough
to pass the color-line that no one would know whom not to put
on the emigration lists. Besides, if all blacks were gone from
America, one suspects it would not relieve white sexual hang-
ups or the white propensity for finding some scapegoat upon
which to unload its frustrations (let what is left of the Amer-

ican Indian populace beware)! Accordingly, since we can't re-
live history, we have no choice but to try and unravel it. This
process might save the nation from itself and get it back on the
track of liberty and equality—a track from which the train
of national hopes got derailed shortly after steaming out of
Independence Hall.

# VIII

# The White Liberal
# as Conservative

A friend of mine recently remarked—and I believe quite cor-
rectly—that the tragedy of the white liberal in our time stems
from the fact that he is really a conservative! He is a conservative because he clings to an idealized vision of American society,
because he more than anyone else recites the national rhetoric
about constitutional guarantees and liberty and justice for all,
and because he stubbornly refuses to acknowledge that most
Americans—Mr. Nixon's "silent majority" if you will—have
already made up their minds that these very principles are
what's basically wrong with the nation. It's the silent majority
that wants to change the Constitution and insists that the problem in America is too much freedom (i.e., permissiveness), especially where blacks and the young are concerned. Constitutional guarantees, so argues the silent majority, have gotten us
nothing except the protection of the criminal at the expense of
the majority of "decent, law-abiding citizens!" And freedom in
this nation, the argument continues, has produced an increasing
crop of young, bearded, unbathed dope addicts, inflated welfare
rolls, and growing lists of draft dodgers. The silent majority
therefore wants change—it pushes for progress into a future
which will be safe and secure because it is firmly entrenched
in white hands—while the liberal finds himself in the awkward
position of longing for the good old days (whenever that was)
when people supposedly believed in the Declaration of Independence, the Constitution, and the Bill of Rights. It is the liberal,
ironically, who wishes to conserve the past, and the silent majority (who have been traditionally accused of being the con-

71

servatives) who seek to press forward into a grand and glorious (i.e., white-dominated) future.

Nothing else explains the dilemma of the white liberal quite as well as this one observation, for in fact the white liberal is the person who is most out of step with the times. When Mr. Nixon appeals to the silent American majority, for example, he clearly does not have the nation's white liberals in mind (to their everlasting credit); his remarks with a consciously calculated cunning are directed toward that segment of the populace which avows everything white liberalism questions: war, increased military expenditures and preparedness, law and order, and a host of similar hallmarks of American patriotism. On the other hand, Vice President Agnew's inanities are directly beamed at white liberalism; when he rails against "effete impudent snobs" and promulgates his "rotten apple" domestic policy, there is little doubt about whom precisely he has in mind.

Consequently, we are faced at this point in American history with the irony of seeing white racists as the champions of change and white liberals as the passionate hold-outs for the way things are theoretically supposed to be. (It may well be that the change which the silent majority wishes is, in fact, a change back to the 19th century, when life was simple, government was small, patriotism ran high and blacks knew their place.) White liberalism, however, finds itself today in a dilemma which it neither fully recognizes nor acknowledges, but one which places it in the embarrassing position of arguing for what it conceives to be the present state of things—a biracial society (which other than in its physical aspects has never existed); integration (which collapsed with the death of Martin Luther King); equal opportunity programs (in which middle-class whites get paid middle-class salaries to tell the poor how bad off they are); and faith in the democratic process (which means that blacks should continue to support liberal whites in election campaigns while whites refuse to return the favor).

This is why, in essence, white liberals turn out to be conservatives at heart. They are conservatives because they hold to an antiquated view of American life which never was and which, in all likelihood, increasingly never will be. They are conservatives because they mistakenly thought that post-World War II developments in race relations were signs of progress, rather than the reluctant reactions of a nation under pressure. Like the Progressive Era liberals at the turn of the present century, they thought that "every day in every way the world was getting a little bit better." Most of all, the white liberal is a conservative because he doesn't listen to the changing mood of the black people whose cause he so devotedly pursues. He has not bothered to notice the resurgence of black self-help and self-determination efforts. He doesn't hear these movements saying that they have grown weary of white assumptions about what's best for the black future, or that black people are determined to "go it alone." The white liberal refuses to believe that blacks have gone sour on integrated schools and neighborhoods; he considers soul food a passing fancy and Afro hair styles a quaint cultural quirk, failing to recognize that, temporary though these cosmetic and culinary delights may be, they too manifest a deeper, more substantive desire to discover that which is authentic about the black experience. The white liberal would never admit it—indeed, he may pale at the suggestion—but his treatment of black attitudes and opinions—his stance which seems to say "I know what's best for blacks whether they recognize it or not"—has all the paternalistic, condescending earmarks of the racism he so richly and righteously denounces!

It's not that white liberalism is necessarily wrong; it's just that white liberals are so dead certain they're right that causes all the confusion. It may well be that when the heat and dust of the present conflict have subsided we'll all wake up to find that white liberalism was right after all, that something did jolt the nation into realizing that its survival as a free and democratic society hinged upon extending economic, social and political freedom to ten percent of its populace and bringing them into the mainstream of the democratic process. But while liberalism clings to this dream with stubborn faith, all the events of contemporary American history are moving in the other direction. Change is taking place in American society, but it is a change toward racial polarization and political repression. Every Gallup poll on the issue of war or welfare reform, the continual flight of whites to suburbia, the dominant mood of the United States Congress, the national policies concocted at 1600 Pennsylvania Avenue in Washington, the election platforms of local politicans—all point to this basic fact of life in America, and liberals should not be blinded to it by their paltry victories in powerless political campaigns in off-year elections. Oddly enough, blacks sense this growing mood in America, and ironically many blacks endorse it. For some it is an inevitable and dramatic way of forcing the black issue in American society, which is why they are prepared to use a strategy of abrasive confrontation to hasten the inevitable. They argue that when white America really shows its true colors (as white Germany did in the thirties vis-à-vis the Jewish people) every black person in the nation will have to get off the dime and join the revolution as a matter of survival. Others see a less dramatic but equally inevitable outcome of the present situation—an emptying of white residents in the city and their replacement by a black populace which can then manipulate the reins of power to its own political, economic and social advantage. But whatever the motive, the fact is that white racists and militant black leadership—the strangest bedfellows in American history—currently find themselves advocating common solutions for the nation's racial ills: both endorse an end to the feeble (and, practically speaking, impossible) attempts to integrate schools, both (albeit for different reasons) are advocates of black self-determination (which in white terms means that it's about time those blacks did something to help themselves), and both, again for different reasons, are united on the issue of turning the cities of the nation over to the blacks (blacks because they think they can run them better and whites because they think the blacks ruined the cities in the first place). The tide of change is sweeping America; both blacks and whites are applauding its direction, and only white liberalism, with its head in the myths of the past, is standing firm, pathetically and at times hysterically trying to hold back the approaching calamity with its dikes of open housing laws and school bussing policies which will crumble like matchsticks once the winds of change reach hurricane force.

Black Americans have been running up the hurricane flags for generations while their white liberal cohorts, economically and socially secure in their own white worlds, have been apathetic to the advancing sounds of diaster. Blacks have looked at Germany in the thirties and at South Africa in the present, and have been continously saying that it could happen in America. White racists have simply smiled at the comparison while white liberals have recoiled in shock at such a suggestion. When the wave of lynchings swept the South in the early sixties, Mississippi inaugurated its systematic program of starvation for blacks in the Delta a few years later, the Minutemen began to mobilize and the John Birch Society started holding seminars all across the nation linking every black social or economic gain with a calculated Communist conspiracy, blacks pleaded with their white liberal cohorts to wake up and recognize what was happening in this country. When George Wallace ran for the presidency of the United States, white liberals applauded the margin of his defeat ("Wasn't it great! He only got ten percent of the vote!") but blacks shuddered at the thought that one out of every ten white Americans could consciously support such madness. Unable, therefore, to convince their few remaining allies that calamity is just around the corner, some blacks have determined, in their words, to "die fighting like men," others are prepared to make a last valiant stand in the supposed strongholds of the nation's cities (which themselves are about as economically and culturally durable as a Kleenex in acid), and still others—and this may come as a profound shock to America's white liberals—have their bags packed and are ready to take the first boat to Canada or the West Indies when the first sound of disaster strikes.

There are still a few black leaders on the national scene who have not lost faith in the biracial future of America, a stand which has earned them the uncoveted label of "Tom" from their more radical black detractors. These leaders head the agencies which have done the most over the years to advance the white liberal dream; their efforts have paved the legal and economic way for integrated schools, limited freedom in the housing market and an integrated black bourgeoisie. At the risk of their jobs, their leadership standing in their own black communities and, on occasion, their lives, these black men have been the most eloquent spokesmen for one America, with blacks and whites living and working side by side in peace and progress. But it is one of the strangest quirks of modern history that these staunch allies of the white liberal hope have been so uniformly deserted by white liberals! The white liberal money, time and effort, which at one time went into making black integrationist agencies a relatively strong force, at least among blacks if not in American society itself, now flows freely into the hands (and pockets) of the black radicals whose gratitude is expressed in loud denunciations of everything white liberalism supposedly holds dear. It is the liberal white who is most knowledgeable (and most vocal) on the subject of the new black leadership, who is so certain about what blacks are thinking and planning, and who, with a passion that escapes either wisdom or common sense, seems most anxious to participate in that process which is calculated to bring about his own ruin. O tempora! O mores! And O the ways of white folks!

There is little wonder that black radicals find themselves content with the currency of white liberals but more content with conversation with the white racists. At least both black radicals and white racists know what they want and where they're going—which is certainly more than can be said for white liberals. White liberalism therefore faces three basic choices: either to square its philosophy with its philanthropy, or (and what might be much more effective) to put its money where its idealistic mouth is, or to opt for a totally new philosophy and strategy which permits it to conserve its ideals and, for the first time in American history, to put some substance behind them. The long view of history would argue that civilization and survival lie with the liberal cause, and that the hopes either of white racists or of black radicals can only lead to cultural collapse and barbarism. It will be all the more tragic, however, if liberalism, by thinking with its heart rather than its head, contributes unwittingly to the very outcome that it historically has sought to avert. Upon white liberalism's coming to its senses therefore may depend not only its own future, but that of the nation as well.

# Epilogue

The basic postulates of the white liberal are that bigotry is caused by ignorance and the changes must be carried out quietly, surreptitiously, as it were, so white people will not notice. These assumptions ignore basic considerations of interest and power and permit white liberals to nibble at the edges of the problem without mounting basic assaults on structures of influence and affluence.

White liberals cannot convert anyone in America until they convert themselves and their constituencies. The first task of the liberal is the creation of a white public and that public cannot be created except by bare-knuckled fights within the ranks of organized labor and organized Christianity.

Lerone Bennett, Jr., *The Negro Mood*

"But what can we do?" This is the plaintive, hand-wringing plea of the nation's decimated ranks of liberals who stand guilt-ridden before the bar of ineffectiveness and who long for a ten-point program which will restore their cause to a state of virtue and influence. Blacks who still talk with whites about race (and those ranks too, by the way, are growing smaller daily) have usually responded to this query by saying, "That's your problem, whitey; you figure it out" (partly because it's true and partly because we're not sure we know the answers either).

Obviously, the problem is too important and the times too critical to permit the luxury of diagnosing an illness for which one is unprepared or unwilling to suggest a cure—a cure which goes beyond merely saying, "Patient, heal thyself," and tries seriously to propose some workable remedy, especially for this most devastating of diseases. In this case, it was suggested earlier that what is needed for patients affected with the disease of racism is nothing short of shock therapy, and by now it should be clear (if there are any white liberal readers still with us) that the therapists are hopefully to be drawn from the ranks of a purged and enlightened white liberalism. The remedy, which may contain much more shock than therapy, suggests simply that we turn both therapist and patient into social revolutionaries, stealing the thunder from the radicals and simultaneously embarking on a sound and substantive program to revolutionize American life and direct it toward ends which are productive and significant for all its people.

# I

There are potentially many people in America who are ripe for such a revolution: old people on fixed incomes, young people who fight the nation's wars but who are excluded from the fruits of its prosperity, dirt farmers and sharecroppers, poor whites and angry blacks, anxious blue collar workers and disgruntled civil servants—these are the people, the majority as a matter of fact, whom this affluent nation cuts off from the benefits of its progress. And American society has gotten away with it as long as it has, mainly by convincing each of these separate segments that its best interest lay in opposing the interests of the others. As long as an aristocratic South could keep poor whites in conflict with blacks, or an affluent North could convince policemen and skilled tradesmen that their worst enemies are unpatriotic youth and the black, urban poor, they could rest secure in the knowledge that all these diverse and disenfranchised elements of American society would never turn on the real centers of power and influence in America—that frightfully small segment of inherited wealth and position which calls the shots and determines the speed and the direction in which this nation moves.

To penetrate and unravel this maze of interlocking directorates which control the future and destiny of the nation, one need not turn the potential of a revolution into the reality of a blood bath, as is mistakenly assumed by that cadre of radical firebrands who are so fervently caught up in contemporary revolutionary rhetoric. This should not and need not happen, especially if revolutionary leadership is drawn from the ranks of religious leadership, that professional guild which above all others in American society is best equipped to bring about a social revolution in this nation. Religious leaders—Jewish, Christian or otherwise—can set themselves to the task of making revolutionaries out of racists, for the tenets of prophetic Judaism and historic Christianity are the best tools for such a job that anyone could possibly ask for.

Priests, pastors and rabbis, therefore, are the potential leaders of the social revolution which America needs, and they can begin their efforts by applying shock therapy to their flocks—the shock of learning that their religious creeds and faiths are, at heart, the most revolutionary message of all times! Actually, the shock should not be too difficult for their hearers, since most church- and synagogue-goers consider themselves unwilling subjects for shock treatment every time they go to Mass or some other service and are bombarded with "social" issues from the pulpit. What may surprise them, however, is to learn that such bombardments are not the wild imaginations of their do-good spiritual leaders but instead the very essence of their religious faiths—a fact which spiritual leaders might have used all along with greater results if American seminaries turned out theologians instead of social workers.

## II

Once before, the makings of such a social revolution were set in motion by the clergy in America. After the Civil War, when cities were new, industrialism was rampant and all the seeds of our present conflict were just beginning to sprout roots, hundreds of religious leaders, fresh from the victory of helping to emancipate some four million slaves, turned their righteous indignation upon "the new slavery" which was no longer chattel but urban and industrial. Appalled by the disease, crime and filth of the cities, and equally incensed by the long hours, unsafe conditions and starvation wages of the sweatshops, these social visionaries were fired by a rediscovery of the social dimensions of their respective faiths (which miraculously they were stumbling upon simultaneously). Catholic, Jewish and Protestant clerics began to denounce the exploitative practices of 19th-century business and industry and to champion the rights of organized labor.* They led assaults on the slums, setting up settlement houses, child care centers, remedial education classes and soup kitchens—all in a valiant attempt to counteract the insipid evils of the robber baron era. They invaded the universities (most of which they already controlled) and created courses and chairs in "Applied Christianity." (The social work profession may not wish to be reminded of the fact that these chairs and courses were the forerunners of its distinguished discipline.) Through their efforts, thousands of college-trained young people were sensitized to the plight of the urban poor and "politicized" into making the relief of these suffering people a lifetime vocation.

Clerics also supported reform candidates for public office and led crusades to clean up corruption in city government. Indeed by 1908, at the first meeting of the Federal Council of Churches, Protestant constituents, under the impact of their awakened social consciousness, had gone so far as to develop a "social creed of the churches," which in part declared the right of workers to be protected from the hardships brought about by industrial change and called for the abolition of child labor, the use of conciliation and arbitration procedures in industrial disputes between workers and management, a reduction in work hours for laborers, a minimum wage scale, equitable distribution of industrial profits and the elimination of poverty.

---

* One of the more renowned Catholic social leaders of the period was Archbishop John Ireland of St. Paul, Minnesota, affectionately known as the "consecrated blizzard of the Northwest."

Today, of course, with the wisdom and perspective that comes from being one hundred years removed from this period, such activity smacks of well-meaning, do-gooder naiveté. Had it not been for such efforts, however, and those that sprang from them in the Progressive and New Deal eras, the plight of the dispossessed in America might be far worse than it is. And though we might call it naiveté today, then it was recognized for what it in essence was: a determined attempt, based upon religious principles and motivated by religious convictions, to achieve the Kingdom of God in America. Its detractors, by the way, called it socialism.

For a host of reasons, the Social Gospel Movement, as it came to be called, declined drastically after World War I. The disillusionment created by the war itself, the disrepute into which liberal theology fell (on which the social activitism of the period rested) after the war, the gradual movement of the reform spirit from the churches into the secular arena where the cudgel was taken up by journalists, an army of social workers, and politicians (who always manage to get in on a good thing when they see it)—all contributed to the collapse of the revolutionary spirit in American religious life. But one of the major reasons for its decline—a reason which should serve as a warning to religious leaders in our own era—was because the social gospel was a cleric's gospel, as the famed editor of *Christian Century* was to note a generation later. The social gospel, in his words, was not "the church's gospel. The laity [had] little share in it."

Much the same onus attaches to white liberal clerics today. They have caught a vision, committed themselves to causes and led crusades to which their flocks are either indifferent or hostile. And instead of becoming the skilled therapist who tries to assess the roots of his patient's illness and then lead that patient toward an effective cure and eventual wholeness, liberal clerics are more likely to develop what in biblical terms might be called an Elijah complex; they flee into the safety of their studies and complain loudly that the world in general and the church in particular is going to hell in a hand basket, and that they, only they, are still among the righteous. When enlightened priests, pastors and rabbis get off their self-righteous kick and take seriously the challenge, impossible though it may seem, to patiently guide their parishioners toward more enlightened and humane attitudes and practices, the revolution will be well under way. And if it takes psychiatrists years of psychoanalytic sessions (at two to three sessions a week) to correct the results of faulty toilet training, pastors surely can exhibit the same professional tolerance for the racist foibles of their flocks.

## III

If the Social Gospel Movement provides the historical precedent for a revolutionary consciousness in this nation, then the movement of the late Martin Luther King—brilliant though brief it may have been—provides the framework and the guidelines for a revolutionary assault upon the inequities of American society in our time. For it was King, more than any other American in this century, who recognized the revolutionary imperative of his religious faith and who, as a preacher, set out to make this nation square its creed with its practices. What separates the successes of King and his movement from the failures of socially-conscious religious institutions and leadership today is that King built his crusade upon a magnificent mass following composed of thousands of Americans committed to the vision of one nation and the technique of non-violence as the most effective tool to bring about the new order in America. The victories of Birmingham and Selma, with their climax in the Civil Rights Acts of 1964 and 1965, and the massive voter registration drives and election successes in Southern communities, therefore, were more than the fruits of one man's leadership and charisma; much more importantly, they were the achievements of the greatest demonstration of black and white commitment to a cause that this nation has ever seen. King accomplished what the Social Gospel Movement never had, and what the liberal-revolutionary movement in contemporary America must have if ever it is to get beyond rapping and rhetoric —a mass following. That following is potentially in the pews of America's churches and synagogues; it can be tapped if the nation's clerics develop the courage, the compassion and the "cool" to turn on their flocks rather than writing them off as a bigoted lost cause.

Revolutionary-minded religionists might also take note of the fact that King was a preacher at heart. His humanistically-inclined admirers tried to ignore the fact and his high-church supporters cringed when they were confronted with it, but the people loved it, and it gave King—with his Baptist fervor, his simple and eloquent language and his unswerving conviction that he was doing God's business—an awesome and powerful appeal to and influence over his people that the arid rationalism of white liberalism or the strident bombast of black radicalism has not been able to equal. King combined in his career what perhaps no other American religious leader has ever been able to effectively achieve—the power of religious faith, a socially sensitive conscience, and guts. Today's clergy, for the most part, suffers from malnutrition in one or more of these vital areas. On the one hand, one finds clerics—many of whom enthusiastically identify with liberal causes and especially with the young—who suffer from acute vocational embarrassment; they are in a constant state of apology (not to be confused with apologetics) for religion's irrelevance, its lack of influence over its members, its hypocrisy, its lack of commitment to critical issues, etc. (as if the American Medical Association, the National Federation of Teachers, the American Bar Association, the American Association of University Professors, the American Federation of Labor and every other professional guild were not afflicted with the same problem). On the other hand, clerics of conservative hue, who sound a continual alarm throughout the nation concerning the perils of sin, the creeping immorality of the times and our nationally uniform need to get back to God, never manage to give the impression that God is interested in anything other than the length (or height?) of mini-skirts, the sale of spirits and intercourse without benefit of license. The sin of urban slums and the immorality of hungry children in the midst of an affluent nation or of war in a thermonuclear age escape them completely.

If the King movement had not been crushed by the assassination of its leader, it might have overcome both these contradictions, giving liberals an opportunity to regain confidence in the efficacy of religion as a revolutionary influence and conservatives a wider set of sins to be concerned with than those associated with short skirts and saloons. With all its flaws and shortcomings, the King movement was as close as we have come to a religiously-inspired revolution in the 20th century. If its fires can be rekindled, its successes enlarged and its mistakes avoided, we may be able to see the dawn of a new era in which this nation finally achieves what it set out to be two hundred years ago—"one nation, under God, indivisible, with liberty and justice for all."

## IV

Revolution, unfortunately, has become a dirty word in the modern American vocabulary; it probably turns off more people than the term "racism." Current usage has been such that when the average citizen hears the word, he thinks of Cubans, Commies (Red or Chinese) or wild-eyed (and -haired) college dropouts, filling the air with four-letter words and endless harangues against an "imperialistic establishment." (Radicals, incidentally, if they are really serious about effecting change—a proposition sometimes open to grave question—would do well to examine their rhetoric and to pick their targets with greater skill and care. What their antics offer in excitement, they frequently lack in elementary common sense, a phenomenon which gives radicals and the United States Vice President an uncommonly similar perspective in mentality and logistics.)

In light of contemporary abhorrence of the term, it is of interest and significance that we still speak proudly of the American and the Industrial Revolutions as triumphal epochs in

American history, or of the scientific and space revolutions as major and beneficial accomplishments in modern life. There is, therefore, an acquaintance with or usage of the word "revolution" in American life (in spite of the fact that it is not to be found in the distinguished dictionary of *American Political Terms*) which makes it apparently acceptable, as long as it works to our political or personal benefit and does not involve our having to give up anything of comfort or value. The problem indeed appears to be not so much with the idea of revolution as it is with a concern about who does the revolting and who will be on top of the national, social and economic heap when it's all over—or, in short, who will win?

If this be the case, then there is indeed hope . . . hope that we can convince the racist who wants change that, given the desire for change, he is already well along the road of the revolutionary spirit; hope also that the racist can be convinced that his best chances for winning lie in the degree to which all of us come out on top, and that therefore he too has a stake in and a reason for joining the great social revolution which this nation must undergo if it is to survive as a free democracy. It will pain the racist to know that he must give up his reactionary attitudes, but he might reluctantly make the sacrifice more willingly if he learns that the radicals will have to necessarily give up their rhetoric, so that all of us—racists, reactionaries, radicals, militants, moderates, Mr. Nixon's "silent majority" and, who knows . . . perhaps even Mr. Nixon himself, especially if he sees a favorable trend developing in the Gallup Poll—can get down to the business of making America a nation of peace and progress.

It is therefore a social revolution which our nation needs, a complete and total change in the way we think and dream and live in American society, a revolution sparked by the religious ideals which every creed in our society affirms, inspired by every religious leader in this country who takes his religion (as opposed to himself) seriously, fed by a determination that no one in America will rest until the words "liberty and justice for all" have become a reality in our national life, and achieved by a massive army of social revolutionists for whom religious faith, social action and the American dream are all interwoven as a single and vital thread in the fabric of our nation's future. Revolution can be a violent overthrow of an existing way of life, but it need not be. However, this much is certain: revolutions have been intimately associated with every period in history in which the ideals of freedom and equality have been taken seriously. Such a period occurred two hundred years ago, and the revolutions to which it gave rise, both in this nation and in Europe, were political and bloody. We have the chance and the challenge, two hundred years later, to direct the unquenchable desire for liberty and justice in America into a revolution that is social and beneficial, not only for every American, but also and ultimately for the entire world. And if we begin this noble task with the proper care, feeding . . . and cure of the white racism in our midst, we may yet all live to enjoy a decent and humane future.